GRE®

POCKET REFERENCE

D0456406

KAPLAN

TEST PREP

Special thanks to the team who made this book possible:

Arthur Ahn, Matthew Belinkie, Shannon Berning, Lauren T. Bernstein, Gerard Cortinez, Elisa Davis, Paula Fleming, Darcy Galane, Joanna Graham, Adam Grey, Adam Hinz, Gar Hong, Xandi Kagstrom, Avi Lidgi, Kate Lopaze, Keith Lubeley, TJ Mancini, Jennifer Moore, Jason Moss, Walt Niedner, Robert Reiss, Derek Rusnak, Emily Sachar, Stephanie Schrauth, Sheryl Stebbins, Glen Stohr, Gene Suhir, Martha P. Torres, Liza Weale, Lee A. Weiss, Emily West, and many others who have contributed materials and advice over the years.

Published by Kaplan Publishing,
a division of Kaplan, Inc.
750 Third Avenue
New York, NY 10017

10 9 8 7

PPN: GG4063E

ISBN: 978-1-62523-482-7

© 2014 Kaplan, Inc.

Contents

PART ONE

Verbal Reference

CHAPTER 1

Kaplan's Word Groups

The following lists contain a lot of common GRE words grouped together by meaning. Make flashcards from these lists and look over your cards a few times a week from now until the day of the test. Look over the word group lists once or twice a week every week until the test. If you don't have much time until the exam date, look over your lists more frequently. Then, by the day of the test, you should have a rough idea of what most of the words on your lists mean.

Note: The categories in which these words are listed are *general* and should *not* be interpreted as the exact definitions of the words.

VERBAL

Abbreviated Communication
abridge
compendium
cursory
curtail
syllabus
synopsis
terse

Act Quickly
abrupt
apace
headlong
impetuous
precipitate

Assist
abet
advocate
ancillary
bolster
corroborate
countenance
espouse
mainstay
munificent
proponent
stalwart
sustenance

Bad Mood
bilious
dudgeon
irascible
pettish
petulant
pique

querulous
umbrage
waspish

Beginner/Amateur
dilettante
fledgling
neophyte
novitiate
proselyte
tyro

Beginning/Young
burgeoning
callow
engender
inchoate
incipient
nascent

Biting
(as in wit or temperament)
acerbic
acidulous
acrimonious
asperity
caustic
mordacious
mordant
trenchant

Bold
audacious
courageous
dauntless

Boring

banal
fatuous
hackneyed
insipid
mundane
pedestrian
platitude
prosaic
quotidian
trite

Carousal

bacchanalian
debauchery
depraved
dissipated
iniquity
libertine
libidinous
licentious
reprobate
ribald
salacious
sordid
turpitude

Changing Quickly

capricious
mercurial
volatile

Copy

counterpart
emulate
facsimile
factitious

paradigm
precursor
quintessence
simulate
vicarious

Criticize/Criticism

aspersion
belittle
berate
calumny
castigate
decry
defame/defamation
denounce
deride/derisive
diatribe
disparage
excoriate
gainsay
harangue
impugn
inveigh
lambaste
objurgate
obloquy
opprobrium
pillory
rebuke
remonstrate
reprehend
reprove
revile
tirade
vituperate

VERBAL

VERBAL

Death/Mourning
bereave
cadaver
defunct
demise
dolorous
elegy
knell
lament
macabre
moribund
obsequies
sepulchral
wraith

Denying of Self
abnegate
abstain
ascetic
spartan
stoic
temperate

Dictatorial
authoritarian
despotic
dogmatic
hegemonic/hegemony
imperious
peremptory
tyrannical

Difficult to Understand
abstruse
ambiguous

arcane
bemusing
cryptic
enigmatic
esoteric
inscrutable
obscure
opaque
paradoxical
perplexing
recondite
turbid

Disgusting/Offensive
defile
fetid
invidious
noisome
odious
putrid
rebarbative

Easy to Understand
articulate
cogent
eloquent
evident
limpid
lucid
pellucid

Eccentric/Dissimilar
aberrant
anachronism
anomalous
discrete
eclectic

esoteric
iconoclast

Embarrass
abash
chagrin
compunction
contrition
diffidence
expiate
foible
gaucherie
rue

Equal
equitable
equity
tantamount

Falsehood
apocryphal
canard
chicanery
dissemble
duplicity
equivocate
erroneous
ersatz
fallacious
feigned
guile
mendacious/mendacity
perfidy
prevaricate
specious
spurious

Family
conjugal
consanguine
distaff
endogamous
filial
fratricide
progenitor
scion

Favoring/Not Impartial
ardent/ardor
doctrinaire
fervid
partisan
tendentious
zealot

Forgive/Make Amends
absolve
acquit
exculpate
exonerate
expiate
palliate
redress
vindicate

Funny
chortle
droll
facetious
flippant
gibe
jocular
levity
ludicrous

VERBAL

VERBAL

raillery
riposte
simper

Gaps/Openings

abatement
aperture
fissure
hiatus
interregnum
interstice
lull
orifice
rent
respite
rift

Generous/Kind

altruistic
beneficent
clement
largess
magnanimous
munificent
philanthropic
unstinting

Greedy

avaricious
covetous
mercenary
miserly
penurious
rapacious
venal

Hard-Hearted

asperity
baleful
dour
fell
malevolent
mordant
sardonic
scathing
truculent
vitriolic
vituperation

Harmful

baleful
baneful
deleterious
inimical
injurious
insidious
minatory
perfidious
pernicious

Harsh-Sounding

cacophony
din
dissonant
raucous
strident

Hatred

abhorrence
anathema
antagonism
antipathy
detestation

enmity
loathing
malice
odium
rancor

Healthy
beneficial
salubrious
salutary

Hesitate
dither
oscillate
teeter
vacillate
waver

Hostile
antithetic
churlish
curmudgeon
irascible
malevolent
misanthropic
truculent
vindictive

Innocent/Inexperienced
credulous
gullible
ingenuous
naive
novitiate
tyro

Insincere
disingenuous
dissemble
fulsome
ostensible
unctuous

Investigate
appraise
ascertain
assay
descry
peruse

Lazy/Sluggish
indolent
inert
lackadaisical
languid
lassitude
lethargic
phlegmatic
quiescent
slothful
torpid

Luck
adventitious
amulet
auspicious
fortuitous
kismet
optimum
portentous
propitiate
propitious
providential

VERBAL

VERBAL

serendipity
talisman

Nag
admonish
belabor
cavil
enjoin
exhort
harangue
hector
martinet
remonstrate
reproof

Nasty
fetid
noisome
noxious

Not a Straight Line
askance
awry
careen
carom
circuitous
circumvent
gyrate
labyrinth
meander
oblique
serrated
sidle
sinuous
undulating
vortex

Overblown/Wordy
bombastic
circumlocution
garrulous
grandiloquent
loquacious
periphrastic
prolix
rhetoric
turgid
verbose

Pacify/Satisfy
ameliorate
appease
assuage
defer
mitigate
mollify
placate
propitiate
satiate
slake
soothe

Pleasant-Sounding
euphonious
harmonious
melodious
sonorous

Poor
destitute
esurient
impecunious
indigent

Praise
   acclaim
   accolade
   aggrandize
   encomium
   eulogize
   extol
   fawn
   laud/laudatory
   venerate/veneration

Predict
   augur
   auspice
   fey
   harbinger
   portentous
   presage
   prescient
   prognosticate

Prevent/Obstruct
   discomfit
   encumber
   fetter
   forfend
   hinder
   impede
   inhibit
   occlude

Smart/Learned
   astute
   canny
   erudite
   perspicacious

Sorrow
   disconsolate
   doleful
   dolor
   elegiac
   forlorn
   lament
   lugubrious
   melancholy
   morose
   plaintive
   threnody

Stubborn
   implacable
   inexorable
   intractable
   intransigent
   obdurate
   obstinate
   recalcitrant
   refractory
   renitent
   untoward
   vexing

Terse
   compendious
   curt
   laconic
   pithy
   succinct
   taciturn

Time/Order/Duration
   anachronism
   antecede

VERBAL

antedate
anterior
archaic
diurnal
eon
ephemeral
epoch
fortnight
millennium
penultimate
synchronous
temporal

Timid/Timidity
craven
diffident
pusillanimous
recreant
timorous
trepidation

Truth
candor/candid
fealty
frankness
indisputable
indubitable
legitimate
probity
sincere
veracious
verity

Unusual
aberration
anomaly
iconoclast
idiosyncrasy

Walking About
ambulatory
itinerant
meander
peripatetic

Wandering
discursive
expatiate
forage
itinerant
peregrination
peripatetic
sojourn

Weaken
adulterate
enervate
exacerbate
inhibit
obviate
stultify
undermine
vitiate

Wisdom
adage
aphorism
apothegm
axiom
bromide
dictum
epigram
platitude
sententious
truism

VERBAL

Withdrawal/Retreat
abeyance
abjure
abnegation
abortive
abrogate
decamp
demur
recant
recidivism
remission
renege
rescind
retrograde

VERBAL

CHAPTER 2

Kaplan's Root List

Kaplan's Root List can boost your knowledge of GRE-level words, and that can help you get more questions right. No one can predict exactly which words will show up on your test, but the testmakers favor certain words. The Root List gives you the component parts of many typical GRE words. Knowing these words can help you because you may run across them on your GRE. Also, becoming comfortable with the types of words that pop up will reduce your anxiety about the test.

Knowing roots can help you in two more ways. First, instead of learning one word at a time, you can learn a whole group of words that contain a certain root. They'll be related in meaning, so if you remember one, it will be easier for you to remember others. Second, roots can often help you decode an unknown GRE word. If you recognize a familiar root, you could get a good enough grasp of the word to answer the question.

This list is a starting point and a quick review, not an exhaustive guide. Roots are given in their most common forms, with their most common or broadest definitions; often, other forms and meanings exist. Similarly, the definitions for the words given as examples may be incomplete, and other senses of those words may exist. Get into the habit of looking up unfamiliar words in a good, current dictionary—whether on paper or on the Internet—and be sure to check their etymologies while you're there.

VERBAL

A/AN: not, without

agnostic: one who believes the existence of God is not provable

amoral: neither moral nor immoral; having no relation to morality

anomaly: an irregularity

anonymous: of unknown authorship or origin

apathy: lack of interest or emotion

atheist: one who does not believe in God

atrophy: the wasting away of body tissue

atypical: not typical

AB: off, away from, apart, down

abdicate: to renounce or relinquish a throne

abduct: to take away by force

abhor: to hate, detest

abject: cast down; degraded

abnormal: deviating from a standard

abolish: to do away with, make void

abstinence: forbearance from any indulgence of appetite

abstract: conceived apart from concrete realities, specific objects, or actual instances

abstruse: hard to understand; secret, hidden

ABLE/IBLE: capable of, worthy of

changeable: able to be changed

combustible: capable of being burned; easily inflamed

inevitable: impossible to be avoided; certain to happen

presentable: suitable for being presented

AC/ACR: sharp, bitter, sour

acerbic: sour or astringent in taste; harsh in temper

acid: something that is sharp, sour, or ill-natured

acrimonious: caustic, stinging, or bitter in nature

acumen: mental sharpness; quickness of wit

acute: sharp at the end; ending in a point

exacerbate: to increase bitterness or violence; aggravate

ACT/AG: to do, to drive, to force, to lead

agile: quick and well-coordinated in movement; active, lively

agitate: to move or force into violent, irregular action

litigate: to make the subject of a lawsuit

pedagogue: a teacher

prodigal: wastefully or recklessly extravagant

synagogue: a gathering or congregation of Jews for the purpose of religious worship

ACOU: hearing

acoustic: pertaining to hearing; sound made through mechanical, not electronic, means

AD: to, toward, near

(Often the *d* is dropped and the first letter to which *a* is prefixed is doubled.)

accede: to yield to a demand; to enter office

adapt: adjust or modify fittingly

addict: to give oneself over, as to a habit or pursuit

address: to direct a speech or written statement to

adhere: to stick fast; cleave; cling

adjacent: near, close, or contiguous; adjoining

adjoin: to be close or in contact with

admire: to regard with wonder, pleasure, and approval

advocate: to plead in favor of

attract: to draw either by physical force or by an appeal to emotions or senses

AL/ALI/ALTER: other, another

alias: an assumed name; another name

alibi: the defense by an accused person that he was verifiably elsewhere at the time of the crime with which he is charged

alien: one born in another country; a foreigner

allegory: figurative treatment of one subject under the guise of another

alter ego: the second self; a substitute or deputy

alternative: a possible choice

altruist: a person unselfishly concerned for the welfare of others

AM: love

amateur: a person who engages in an activity for pleasure rather than financial or professional gain

amatory: of or pertaining to lovers or lovemaking

amiable: having or showing agreeable personal qualities

amicable: characterized by exhibiting good will

amity: friendship; peaceful harmony

amorous: inclined to love, esp. sexual love

enamored: inflamed with love; charmed; captivated

inamorata: a female lover

VERBAL

VERBAL

AMBI/AMPHI: both, on both sides, around

ambidextrous: able to use both hands equally well

ambient: moving around freely; circulating

ambiguous: open to various interpretations

amphibian: any cold-blooded vertebrate, the larva of which is aquatic and the adult of which is terrestrial; a person or thing having a twofold nature

AMBL/AMBUL: to go, to walk

ambulance: a vehicle equipped for carrying sick people (from a phrase meaning "walking hospital")

ambulatory: of, pertaining to, or capable of walking

perambulator: one who makes a tour of inspection on foot

preamble: an introductory statement (originally: to walk in front)

ANIM: of the life, mind, soul, breath

animal: a living being

animosity: a feeling of ill will or enmity

equanimity: mental or emotional stability, especially under tension

magnanimous: generous in forgiving an insult or injury

unanimous: of one mind; in complete accord

ANNUI/ENNI: year

annals: a record of events, esp. a yearly record

anniversary: the yearly recurrence of the date of a past event

annual: of, for, or pertaining to a year; yearly

annuity: a specified income payable at stated intervals

perennial: lasting for an indefinite amount of time

ANT/ANTE: before

antebellum: before the war (especially the American Civil War)

antecedent: existing, being, or going before

antedate: precede in time

antediluvian: belonging to the period before the biblical flood; very old or old-fashioned

anterior: placed before

ANTHRO/ANDR: man, human

androgen: any substance that promotes masculine characteristics

androgynous: being both male and female

android: robot; mechanical man

anthropocentric: regarding humanity as the central fact of the universe

anthropology: the science that deals with the origins of humankind

misanthrope: one who hates humans or humanity

philanderer: one who carries on flirtations

ANTI: against, opposite

antibody: a protein naturally existing in blood serum that reacts to overcome the toxic effects of an antigen

antidote: a remedy for counteracting the effects of poison, disease, etc.

antipathy: aversion

antipodal: on the opposite side of the globe

antiseptic: free from germs; particularly clean or neat

APO: away

apocalypse: revelation; discovery; disclosure

apocryphal: of doubtful authorship or authenticity

apogee: the highest or most distant point

apology: an expression of one's regret or sorrow for having wronged another

apostasy: a total desertion of one's religion, principles, party, cause, etc.

apostle: one of the 12 disciples sent forth by Jesus to preach the Gospel

AQUA/AQUE: water

aquamarine: a bluish-green color

aquarium: a tank for keeping fish and other underwater creatures

aquatic: having to do with water

aqueduct: a channel for transporting water

subaqueous: underwater

ARCH/ARCHI/ARCHY: chief, principal, ruler

anarchy: a state or society without government or law

archenemy: chief enemy

architect: the devisor, maker, or planner of anything

monarchy: a government in which the supreme power is lodged in a sovereign

oligarchy: a state or society ruled by a select group

ARD: to burn

ardent: burning; fierce; passionate

ardor: flame; passion

arson: the crime of setting property on fire

AUTO: self

autocrat: an absolute ruler

automatic: self-moving or self-acting

autonomy: independence or freedom

BE: about, to make, to surround, to affect (often used to transform words into transitive verbs)

belie: to misrepresent; to contradict

belittle: to make small; to make something appear smaller

bemoan: to moan for; to lament

bewilder: to confuse completely (that is, to make one mentally wander)

BEL/BELL: beautiful

belle: a beautiful woman

embellish: to make beautiful; to ornament

BELL: war

antebellum: before the war (especially the American Civil War)

belligerent: warlike, given to waging war

rebel: a person who resists authority, control, or tradition

BEN/BENE: good

benediction: act of uttering a blessing

benefit: anything advantageous to a person or thing

benevolent: desiring to do good to others

benign: having a kindly disposition

BI/BIN: two

biennial: happening every two years

bilateral: pertaining to or affecting two or both sides

bilingual: able to speak one's native language and another with equal facility

binocular: involving two eyes

bipartisan: representing two parties

combination: the joining of two or more things into a whole

BON/BOUN: good, generous

bona fide: in good faith; without fraud

bonus: something given over and above what is due

bountiful: generous

BREV/BRID: short, small

abbreviate: to shorten

abridge: to shorten

brevet: an honorary promotion with no additional pay

VERBAL

breviloquent: laconic; concise in one's speech

brevity: shortness

brief: short

BURS: purse, money

bursar: treasurer

bursary: treasury

disburse: to pay

reimburse: to pay back

CAD/CID: to fall, to happen by chance

accident: happening by chance; unexpected

cascade: a waterfall descending over a steep surface

coincidence: a striking occurrence of two or more events at one time, apparently by chance

decadent: decaying; deteriorating

recidivist: one who repeatedly relapses, as into crime

CANT/CENT/CHANT: to sing

accent: prominence of a syllable in terms of pronunciation

chant: a song; singing

enchant: to subject to magical influence; bewitch

incantation: the chanting of words purporting to have magical power

incentive: that which incites action

recant: to withdraw or disavow a statement

CAP/CIP/CEPT: to take, to get

anticipate: to realize beforehand; foretaste or foresee

capture: to take by force or stratagem

emancipate: to free from restraint

percipient: having perception; discerning; discriminating

precept: a commandment or direction given as a rule of conduct

susceptible: capable of receiving, admitting, undergoing, or being affected by something

CAP/CAPIT/CIPIT: head, headlong

capital: the city or town that is the official seat of government

capitulate: to surrender unconditionally or on stipulated terms

caption: a heading or title

disciple: one who is a pupil of the doctrines of another

precipice: a cliff with a vertical face

precipitate: to hasten the occurrence of; to bring about prematurely

VERBAL

VERBAL

CARD/CORD/COUR: heart

cardiac: pertaining to the heart

concord: agreement; peace, amity

concordance: agreement, concord, harmony

discord: lack of harmony between persons or things

encourage: to inspire with spirit or confidence

CARN: flesh

carnage: the slaughter of a great number of people

carnival: a traveling amusement show

carnivorous: eating flesh

incarnation: a being invested with a bodily form

reincarnation: rebirth of a soul in a new body

CAST/CHAST: to cut

cast: to throw or hurl; fling

caste: a hereditary social group, limited to people of the same rank

castigate: to punish in order to correct

chaste: free from obscenity; decent

chastise: to discipline, esp. by corporal punishment

CAUS/CAUT: to burn

caustic: burning or corrosive

cauterize: to burn or deaden

cautery: an instrument used for branding; branding

holocaust: a burnt offering; complete destruction by fire or other means

CED/CEED/CESS: to go, to yield, to stop

accede: to yield to a demand; to enter office

antecedent: existing, being, or going before

cessation: a temporary or complete discontinuance

concede: to acknowledge as true, just, or proper; admit

incessant: without stop

predecessor: one who comes before another in an office, position, etc.

CELER: speed

accelerant: something used to speed up a process

accelerate: to increase in speed

celerity: speed; quickness

decelerate: to decrease in speed

CENT: hundred, hundredth

bicentennial: two-hundredth anniversary

cent: a hundredth of a dollar

centigrade: a temperature system with one hundred degrees between the freezing and boiling points of water

centimeter: one hundredth of
a meter
centipede: a creature with many
legs
century: one hundred years
percent: in every hundred

CENTR: center
centrifuge: an apparatus that
rotates at high speed and
separates substances of
different densities using
centrifugal force
centrist: of or pertaining to
moderate political or social
ideas
concentrate: to bring to a common center; to converge, to
direct toward one point
concentric: having a com-
mon center, as in circles or
spheres
eccentric: off-center

CERN/CERT/CRET/CRIM/ CRIT: to separate, to judge, to distinguish, to decide
ascertain: to make sure of; to
determine
certitude: freedom from doubt
criterion: a standard of judgment or criticism
discreet: judicious in one's
conduct of speech, esp.
with regard to maintaining
silence about something of a
delicate nature

discrete: detached from others,
separate
hypocrite: a person who pre-
tends to have beliefs that she
does not

CHROM: color
chromatic: having to do with
color
chrome: a metallic element
(chromium) used to make
vivid colors or something
plated with chromium
chromosome: genetic material
that can be studied by coloring it with dyes
monochromatic: having only
one color

CHRON: time
anachronism: something that is
out-of-date or belonging to
the wrong time
chronic: constant, habitual
chronology: the sequential
order in which past events
occurred
chronometer: a highly accurate
clock or watch
synchronize: to occur at the
same time or agree in time

CIRCU/CIRCUM: around
circuit: a line around an area; a
racecourse; the path traveled
by electrical current
circuitous: roundabout, indirect

VERBAL

circumference: the outer boundary of a circular area

circumspect: cautious; watching all sides

circumstances: the existing conditions or state of affairs surrounding and affecting an agent

CIS: to cut

exorcise: to seek to expel an evil spirit by ceremony

incision: a cut, gash, or notch

incisive: penetrating, cutting

precise: definitely stated or defined

scissors: cutting instrument for paper

CLA/CLO/CLU: to shut, to close

claustrophobia: an abnormal fear of enclosed places

cloister: a courtyard bordered with covered walks, esp. in a religious institution

conclude: to bring to an end; finish; to terminate

disclose: to make known, reveal, or uncover

exclusive: not admitting of something else; shutting out others

preclude: to prevent the presence, existence, or occurrence of

CLAIM/CLAM: to shout, to cry out

clamor: a loud uproar

disclaim: to deny interest in or connection with

exclaim: to cry out or speak suddenly and vehemently

proclaim: to announce or declare in an official way

reclaim: to claim or demand the return of a right or possession

CLI: to lean toward

climax: the most intense point in the development of something

decline: to cause to slope or incline downward

disinclination: aversion, distaste

proclivity: inclination, bias

recline: to lean back

CO/COL/COM/CON: with, together

coerce: to compel by force, intimidation, or authority

collaborate: to work with another, cooperate

collide: to strike one another with a forceful impact

commensurate: suitable in measure, proportionate

compatible: capable of existing together in harmony

conciliate: to placate, win over

connect: to bind or fasten together

COGN/CONN: to know

cognition: the process of knowing

incognito: with one's name or identity concealed

recognize: to identify as already known

CONTRA/CONTRO/COUNTER: against

contradict: to oppose; to speak against

contrary: opposed to; opposite

controversy: a disputation; a quarrel

counterfeit: fake; a false imitation

countermand: to retract an order

encounter: a meeting, often with an opponent

CORP/CORS: body

corporation: a company legally treated as an individual

corps: a body (an organized group) of troops

corpse: a dead body

corpulent: obese; having a lot of flesh

corset: a garment used to give shape and support to the body

incorporation: combining into a single body

COSM: order, universe, world

cosmetic: improving the appearance (making it look better ordered)

cosmic: relating to the universe

cosmology: a theory of the universe as a whole

cosmonaut: an astronaut; an explorer of outer space

cosmopolitan: worldly

cosmos: the universe; an orderly system; order

microcosm: a small system that reflects a larger whole

COUR/CUR: running, a course

concur: to accord in opinion; agree

courier: a messenger traveling in haste who bears news

curriculum: the regular course of study

cursive: handwriting in flowing strokes with the letters joined together

cursory: going rapidly over something; hasty; superficial

excursion: a short journey or trip

incursion: a hostile entrance into a place, esp. suddenly

recur: to happen again

CRE/CRESC/CRET: to grow

accretion: an increase by natural growth

VERBAL

accrue: to be added as a matter of periodic gain

creation: the act of producing or causing to exist

excrescence: an outgrowth

increase: to make greater in any respect

increment: something added or gained; an addition or increase

CRED: to believe, to trust

credentials: anything that provides the basis for belief

credit: trustworthiness

credo: any formula of belief

credulity: willingness to believe or trust too readily

incredible: unbelievable

CRYPT: hidden

apocryphal: of doubtful authorship or authenticity

crypt: a subterranean chamber or vault

cryptography: procedures of making and using secret writing

cryptology: the science of interpreting secret writings, codes, ciphers, and the like

CUB/CUMB: to lie down

cubicle: any small space or compartment that is partitioned off

incubate: to sit upon for the purpose of hatching

incumbent: holding an indicated position

recumbent: lying down; reclining; leaning

succumb: to give away to superior force; yield

CULP: fault, blame

culpable: deserving blame or censure

culprit: a person guilty of an offense

inculpate: to charge with fault

mea culpa: through my fault; my fault

DAC/DOC: to teach

didactic: intended for instruction

docile: easily managed or handled; tractable

doctor: someone licensed to practice medicine; a learned person

doctrine: a particular principle advocated, as of a government or religion

indoctrinate: to imbue a person with learning

DE: away, off, down, completely, reversal

decipher: to make out the meaning; to interpret

defame: to attack the good name or reputation of

deferential: respectful; to yield to judgment

defile: to make foul, dirty, or unclean

delineate: to trace the outline of; sketch or trace in outline

descend: to move from a higher to a lower place

DELE: to erase

delete: erase; blot out; remove

indelible: impossible to erase; lasting

DEM: people

democracy: government by the people

demographics: vital and social statistics of populations

endemic: peculiar to a particular people or locality

epidemic: affecting a large number of people at the same time and spreading from person to person

pandemic: general, universal

DEXT: right hand, right side, deft

ambidextrous: equally able to use both hands

dexter: on the right

dexterity: deftness; adroitness

DI: day

dial: a device for seeing the hour of the day; a clock face; rotatable discs or knobs used as a control input

diary: a record of one's days

dismal: gloomy (from "bad days")

diurnal: daily

meridian: a direct line from the North Pole to the South Pole; the highest point reached by the sun; noon

quotidian: everyday; ordinary

DI/DIA: in two, through, across

diagnose: to identify disease or fault from symptoms

dialogue: conversation between two or more persons

diameter: a line going through a circle, dividing it in two

dichotomy: division into two parts, kinds, etc.

DI/DIF/DIS: away from, apart, reversal, not

diffuse: to pour out and spread, as in a fluid

dilate: to make wider or larger; to cause to expand

dilatory: inclined to delay or procrastinate

disperse: to drive or send off in various directions

VERBAL

VERBAL

disseminate: to scatter or spread widely; promulgate

dissipate: to scatter wastefully

dissuade: to deter by advice or persuasion

DIC/DICT/DIT: to say, to tell, to use words

dictionary: a book containing a selection of the words of a language

interdict: to forbid; prohibit

predict: to tell in advance

verdict: a judgment or decision

DIGN: worth

condign: well deserved; fitting; adequate

deign: to think fit or in accordance with one's dignity

dignitary: a person who holds a high rank or office

dignity: nobility or elevation of character; worthiness

disdain: to look upon or treat with contempt

DOG/DOX: opinion

dogma: a system of tenets, as of a church

orthodox: sound or correct in opinion or doctrine

paradox: an opinion or statement contrary to accepted opinion

DOL: to suffer, to pain, to grieve

condolence: expression of sympathy with one who is suffering

doleful: sorrowful, mournful

dolorous: full of pain or sorrow, grievous

indolence: a state of being lazy or slothful

DON/DOT/DOW: to give

anecdote: a short narrative about an interesting event

antidote: something that prevents or counteracts ill effects

donate: to present as a gift or contribution

endow: to provide with a permanent fund

pardon: kind indulgence, forgiveness

DORM: sleep

dormant: sleeping; inactive

dormitory: a place for sleeping; a residence hall

DORS: back

dorsal: having to do with the back

endorse: to sign on the back; to vouch for

DUB: doubt

dubiety: doubtfulness

dubious: doubtful
indubitable: unquestionable

DUC/DUCT: to lead
abduct: to carry off or lead away
conducive: contributive, helpful
conduct: personal behavior, way of acting
induce: to lead or move by influence
induct: to install in a position with formal ceremonies
produce: to bring into existence; give cause to

DULC: sweet
dulcet: sweet; pleasing
dulcified: sweetened; softened
dulcimer: a musical instrument

DUR: hard, lasting
dour: sullen, gloomy (originally: hard, obstinate)
durable: able to resist decay
duration: the length of time something exists
duress: compulsion by threat, coercion
endure: to hold out against; to sustain without yielding
obdurate: stubborn, resistant to persuasion

DYS: faulty, abnormal
dysfunctional: poorly functioning

dyslexia: an impairment of the ability to read due to a brain defect
dyspepsia: impaired digestion
dystrophy: faulty or inadequate nutrition or development

E/EX: out, out of, from, former, completely
efface: to rub or wipe out; surpass, eclipse
evade: to escape from, avoid
exclude: to shut out; to leave out
exonerate: to free or declare free from blame
expire: to breathe out; to breathe one's last; to end
extricate: to disentangle, release

EGO: self
ego: oneself; the part of oneself that is self-aware
egocentric: focused on oneself
egoism/egotism: selfishness; self-absorption

EM/EN: in, into
embrace: to clasp in the arms; to include or contain
enclose: to close in on all sides

EPI: upon
epidemic: affecting a large number of people at the same time and spreading from person to person

VERBAL

VERBAL

epidermis: the outer layer of the skin

epigram: a witty or pointed saying tersely expressed

epilogue: a concluding part added to a literary work

epithet: a word or phrase, used invectively as a term of abuse

EQU: equal, even

adequate: equal to the requirement or occasion

equation: the act of making equal

equidistant: equally distant

iniquity: gross injustice; wickedness

ERR: to wander

arrant: notorious; downright (originally: wandering)

err: to go astray in thought or belief, to be mistaken

erratic: deviating from the proper or usual course in conduct

error: a deviation from accuracy or correctness

ESCE: becoming

adolescent: between childhood and adulthood

convalescent: recovering from illness

incandescent: glowing with heat, shining

obsolescent: becoming obsolete

reminiscent: reminding or suggestive of

EU: good, well

eugenics: improvement of qualities of race by control of inherited characteristics

eulogy: speech or writing in praise or commendation

euphemism: pleasant-sounding term for something unpleasant

euphony: pleasantness of sound

euthanasia: killing a person painlessly, usually one who has an incurable, painful disease

EXTRA: outside, beyond

extract: to take out, obtain against a person's will

extradite: to hand over (person accused of crime) to state where crime was committed

extraordinary: beyond the ordinary

extrapolate: to estimate (unknown facts or values) from known data

extrasensory: derived by means other than known senses

FAB/FAM: to speak

affable: friendly, courteous

defame: to attack the good name of

fable: fictional tale, esp. legendary

famous: well known, celebrated

ineffable: too great for description in words; that which must not be uttered

FAC/FIC/FIG/FAIT/FEIT/FY: to do, to make

configuration: manner of arrangement, shape

counterfeit: imitation, forgery

deficient: incomplete or insufficient

effigy: sculpture or model of person

faction: small dissenting group within larger one, esp. in politics

factory: building for manufacture of goods

prolific: producing many offspring or much output

ratify: to confirm or accept by formal consent

FAL: to err, to deceive

default: to fail

fail: to be insufficient; to be unsuccessful; to die out

fallacy: a flawed argument

false: not true; erroneous; lying

faux pas: a false step; a social gaffe

infallible: incapable of being wrong or being deceived

FATU: foolish

fatuity: foolishness; stupidity

fatuous: foolish; stupid

infatuated: swept up in a fit of passion, impairing one's reason

FER: to bring, to carry, to bear

confer: to grant, bestow

offer: to present for acceptance, refusal, or consideration

proffer: to offer

proliferate: to reproduce; produce rapidly

referendum: to vote on political question open to the entire electorate

FERV: to boil, to bubble

effervescent: with the quality of giving off bubbles of gas

fervid: ardent, intense

fervor: passion, zeal

FI/FID: faith, trust

affidavit: written statement on oath

confide: to entrust with a secret

fidelity: faithfulness, loyalty

fiduciary: of a trust; held or given in trust

infidel: disbeliever in the supposed true religion

VERBAL

VERBAL

FIN: end

confine: to keep or restrict within certain limits; imprison

definitive: decisive, unconditional, final

final: at the end; coming last

infinite: boundless; endless

infinitesimal: infinitely or very small

FLAGR/FLAM: to burn

conflagration: a large, destructive fire

flagrant: blatant, scandalous

flambeau: a lighted torch

inflame: to set on fire

FLECT/FLEX: to bend, to turn

deflect: to bend or turn aside from a purpose

flexible: able to bend without breaking

genuflect: to bend knee, esp. in worship

inflect: to change or vary pitch of

reflect: to throw back

FLU/FLUX: to flow

confluence: merging into one

effluence: flowing out of (light, electricity, etc.)

fluctuation: something that varies, rising and falling

fluid: substance, esp. gas or liquid, capable of flowing freely

mellifluous: pleasing, musical

FORE: before

foreshadow: be warning or indication of (future event)

foresight: care or provision for future

forestall: to prevent by advance action

forthright: straightforward, outspoken, decisive

FORT: chance

fortuitous: happening by luck

fortunate: lucky, auspicious

fortune: chance or luck in human affairs

FORT: strength

forte: strong point; something a person does well

fortify: to provide with fortifications; strengthen

fortissimo: very loud

FRA/FRAC/FRAG/FRING: to break

fractious: irritable, peevish

fracture: breakage, esp. of a bone

fragment: a part broken off

infringe: to break or violate (a law, etc.)

refractory: stubborn, unmanageable, rebellious

FUG: to flee, to fly

centrifugal: flying off from the center

fugitive: on the run; someone who flees

fugue: a musical composition in which subsequent parts imitate or pursue the first part; a psychological state in which one flies from one's own identity

refuge: a haven for those fleeing

refugee: a fleeing person who seeks refuge

subterfuge: a deception used to avoid a confrontation

FULG: to shine

effulgent: shining forth

refulgent: radiant; shining

FUM: smoke

fume: smoke; scented vapor; to emit smoke or vapors

fumigate: to treat with smoke or vapors

perfume: scents, from burning incense or other sources of fragrance

FUS: to pour

diffuse: to spread widely or thinly

fusillade: continuous discharge of firearms or outburst of criticism

infusion: the act of permeating or steeping; liquid extract so obtained

profuse: lavish, extravagant, copious

suffuse: to spread throughout or over from within

GEN: birth, creation, race, kind

carcinogenic: producing cancer

congenital: existing or as such from birth

gender: classification roughly corresponding to the two sexes and sexlessness

generous: giving or given freely

genetics: study of heredity and variation among animals and plants

progeny: offspring, descendants

GN/GNO: to know

agnostic: one who believes that the existence of God is not provable

diagnose: to identify disease or fault from symptoms

ignoramus: a person lacking knowledge, uninformed

ignore: to refuse to take notice of

prognosis: to forecast, especially of disease

VERBAL

GRAD/GRESS: to step

aggressive: given to hostile act or feeling

degrade: to humiliate, dishonor, reduce to lower rank

digress: to depart from main subject

egress: going out; way out

progress: forward movement

regress: to move backward, revert to an earlier state

GRAM/GRAPH: to write, to draw

diagram: a figure made by drawing lines; an illustration

epigram: a short poem; a pointed statement

grammar: a system of language and its rules

graph: a diagram used to convey mathematical information

graphite: mineral used for writing, as the "lead" in pencils

photograph: a picture, originally made by exposing chemically treated film to light

GRAT: pleasing

gracious: kindly, esp. to inferiors; merciful

grateful: thankful

gratuity: money given for good service

ingratiate: to bring oneself into favor

GREG: flock

aggregate: a number of things considered as a collective whole

congregate: to come together in a group

egregious: remarkably bad; standing out from the crowd

gregarious: sociable; enjoying spending time with others

segregate: to separate from the crowd

HAP: by chance

haphazard: at random

hapless: without luck

happen: occur (originally: to occur by chance)

happily: through good fortune

happy: pleased, as by good fortune

mishap: an unlucky accident

perhaps: a qualifier suggesting something might (or might not) take place

HEMI: half

hemisphere: half a sphere; half of the Earth

hemistich: half a line of poetry

HER/HES: to stick

adherent: able to adhere; believer or advocate of a particular thing adhesive: tending to remain in memory; sticky; an adhesive substance

coherent: logically consistent; having waves in phase and of one wavelength

inherent: involved in the constitution or essential character of something

(H)ETERO: different, other

heterodox: different from acknowledged standard; holding unorthodox opinions or doctrines

heterogeneous: of other origin; not originating in the body

heterosexual: of or pertaining to sexual orientation toward members of the opposite sex; relating to different sexes

HOL: whole

catholic: universal

holocaust: a burnt offering; complete destruction by fire or other means

hologram: a sort of three-dimensional image

holograph: a document written entirely by the person whose name it's in

holistic: considering something as a unified whole

(H)OM: same

anomaly: deviation from the common rule

homeostasis: a relatively stable state of equilibrium

homogeneous: of the same or a similar kind of nature; of uniform structure of composition throughout

homonym: one of two or more words spelled and pronounced alike but different in meaning

homosexual: of, relating to, or exhibiting sexual desire toward a member of one's own sex

HUM: earth

exhume: unearth

humble: down-to-earth

humility: the state of being humble

HYPER: over, excessive

hyperactive: excessively active

hyperbole: purposeful exaggeration for effect

hyperglycemia: an abnormally high concentration of sugar in the blood

HYPO: under, beneath, less than

hypochondriac: one affected by extreme depression of mind

VERBAL

or spirits, often centered on imaginary physical ailments

hypocritical: pretending to have beliefs one does not

hypodermic: relating to the parts beneath the skin

hypothesis: assumption subject to proof

ICON: image, idol

icon: a symbolic picture; a statue; something seen as representative of a culture or movement

iconic: being representative of a culture or movement

iconoclast: one who attacks established beliefs; one who tears down images

iconology: symbolism

IDIO: one's own

idiom: a language, dialect, or style of speaking particular to a people

idiosyncrasy: peculiarity of temperament; eccentricity

idiot: an utterly stupid person

IN/IM: not, without

(Often the *m* is dropped and the first letter to which *i* is prefixed is doubled.)

immoral: not moral; evil

impartial: not partial or biased; just

inactive: not active

indigent: deficient in what is requisite

indolence: showing a disposition to avoid exertion; slothful

innocuous: not harmful or injurious

IN/IM: in, into

(Often the *m* is dropped and the first letter to which *i* is prefixed is doubled.)

implicit: not expressly stated; implied

incarnate: given a bodily, esp. a human, form

indigenous: native; innate, natural

influx: the act of flowing in; inflow

intrinsic: belonging to a thing by its very nature

INTER: between, among

interim: a temporary or provisional arrangement; meantime

interloper: one who intrudes in the domain of others

intermittent: stopping or ceasing for a time

intersperse: to scatter here and there

interstate: connecting or jointly involving states

VERBAL

INTRA: inside, within

intramural: within a school; inside a city

intrastate: within a state

intravenous: inside the veins

IT/ITER: way, journey

ambition: strong desire to achieve (from "going around" for votes)

circuit: a line around an area; a racecourse; the path traveled by electrical current

itinerant: traveling

itinerary: travel plans

reiterate: to repeat

transit: traveling; means of transportation

JECT: to throw, to throw down

abject: utterly hopeless, humiliating, or wretched

conjecture: formation of opinion on incomplete information

dejected: sad, depressed

eject: to throw out, expel

inject: to place (quality, etc.) where needed in something

JOC: joke

jocose: given to joking; playful

jocular: in a joking manner; funny

jocund: merry; cheerful

joke: a witticism; a humorous anecdote; something funny

JOIN/JUG/JUNCT: to meet, to join

adjoin: to be next to and joined with

conjugal: related to marriage

conjunction: joining; occurring together; a connecting word

injunction: a command; an act of enjoining

junction: the act of joining; combining; a place where multiple paths join

junta: a group of military officers who join together to run a country; a council

rejoinder: to reply, retort

subjugate: to make subservient; to place under a yoke

JOUR: day

adjourn: to close a meeting; to put off further proceedings for another day

journal: a record of one's days

journey: a trip (originally: a day's travel)

JUD: to judge

adjudicate: to act as a judge

judiciary: a system of courts; members of a court system

judicious: having good judgment

prejudice: a previous or premature judgment; bias

VERBAL

JUR: law, to swear

abjure: to renounce on oath
adjure: to beg or command
jurisprudence: a system of law; knowledge of law
perjury: willful lying while on oath

JUV: young

juvenile: young; immature
juvenilia: writings or art produced in one's youth
rejuvenate: to refresh; to make young again

LANG/LING: tongue

bilingual: speaking two languages
language: a system of (usually spoken) communication
linguistics: the study of language

LAUD: praise, honor

cum laude: with honors
laudable: praiseworthy
laudatory: expressing praise

LAV/LAU/LU: to wash

ablution: act of cleansing
antediluvian: before the biblical flood; extremely old
deluge: a great flood of water
dilute: to make thinner or weaker by the addition of water

laundry: items to be, or that have been, washed
lavatory: a room with equipment for washing hands and face

LAX/LEAS/LES: loose

lax: loose; undisciplined
laxative: medicine or food that loosens the bowels
lease: to rent out (that is, to let something loose for others' use)
leash: a cord used to hold an animal while giving it some freedom to run loose
relax: loosen; be less strict; calm down
release: let go; set free

LEC/LEG/LEX: to read, to speak

dialect: a manner of speaking; a regional variety of a language
lectern: a reading desk
lecture: an instructional speech
legend: a story; a written explanation of a map or illustration
legible: readable
lesson: instruction (originally: part of a book or oral instruction to be studied and repeated to a teacher)
lexicographer: a writer of dictionaries
lexicon: dictionary

VERBAL

LECT/LEG: to select, to choose

collect: to gather together or assemble

eclectic: selecting ideas, etc. from various sources

elect: to choose; to decide

predilection: preference, liking

select: to choose with care

LEV: to lift, to rise, light (weight)

alleviate: to make easier to endure, lessen

levee: embankment against river flooding

levitate: to rise in the air or cause to rise

levity: humor, frivolity, gaiety

relevant: bearing on or pertinent to information at hand

relieve: to mitigate; to free from a burden

LI/LIG: to tie, to bind

ally: to unite; one in an alliance

league: an association; a group of nations, teams, etc. that have agreed to work for a common cause

liable: legally responsible; bound by law

liaison: a connection; one who serves to connect

lien: the right to hold a property due to an outstanding debt

ligament: a band holding bones together; a bond

ligature: a connection between two letters; a bond

oblige: to obligate; to make indebted or form personal bonds by doing a favor

rely: to depend upon (originally: to come together; to rally)

LIBER: free

deliver: to set free; to save; to hand over

liberal: generous; giving away freely

liberality: generosity

liberate: set free

libertine: one who follows one's own path, without regard for morals or other restrictions

liberty: freedom

livery: a uniform; an emblem indicating an owner or manufacturer (originally: an allowance of food or other provisions given to servants)

LITH: stone

acrolith: a statue with a stone head and limbs (but a wooden body)

lithography: a printing process that originally involved writing on a flat stone

lithology: the study of rocks and stones

lithotomy: an operation to remove stones from the body

VERBAL

megalith: a very big stone
monolith: a single block of
stone, often shaped into a
monument

LOC/LOG/LOQU: word, speech, thought

colloquial: of ordinary or familiar conversation
dialogue: conversation, esp. in a literary work
elocution: art of clear and expressive speaking
eulogy: speech or writing in praise of someone
grandiloquent: pompous or inflated in language
loquacious: talkative
prologue: introduction to poem, play, etc.

LUC/LUM/LUS: light (brightness)

illuminate: to supply or brighten with light
illustrate: to make intelligible with examples or analogies
illustrious: highly distinguished
lackluster: lacking brilliance or radiance
lucid: easily understood, intelligible
luminous: bright, brilliant, glowing
translucent: permitting light to pass through

LUD/LUS: to play

allude: to refer casually or indirectly
delude: to mislead the mind or judgment of, deceive
elude: to avoid capture or escape defection by
illusion: something that deceives by producing a false impression of reality
ludicrous: ridiculous, laughable
prelude: a preliminary to an action, event, etc.

MACRO: great, long

macro: broad; large; a single computer command that executes a longer set of commands
macrobiotics: a system intended to prolong life
macrocephalous: having a large head
macrocosm: the universe; a large system that is reflected in at least one of its subsets
macroscopic: large enough to be visible to the naked eye

MAG/MAJ/MAX: big, great

magnanimous: generous in forgiving an insult or injury
magnate: a powerful or influential person
magnify: to increase the apparent size of

magnitude: greatness of size, extent, or dimensions

maxim: an expression of general truth or principle

maximum: the highest amount, value, or degree attained

MAL/MALE: bad, ill, evil, wrong

maladroit: clumsy, tactless

malady: a disorder or disease of the body

malapropism: humorous misuse of a word

malediction: a curse

malfeasance: misconduct or wrongdoing often committed by a public official

malfunction: failure to function properly

malicious: full of or showing malice

malign: to speak harmful untruths about, to slander

MAN/MANU: hand

emancipate: to free from bondage

manifest: readily perceived by the eye or the understanding

manual: operated by hand

manufacture: to make by hand or machinery

MAND/MEND: to command, to order, to entrust

command: to order; an order; control

commend: to give something over to the care of another; to praise

countermand: to retract an order

demand: to strongly ask for; to claim; to require

mandatory: commanded; required

recommend: to praise and suggest the use of; to advise

remand: to send back

MEDI: middle

immediate: nearest; having nothing in between

intermediate: in the middle

mean: average; in the middle

mediate: to serve as a go-between; to try to settle an argument

medieval: related to the Middle Ages

mediocre: neither good nor bad; so-so

medium: size between small and large; a substance or agency that things travel through (as, for example, light travels through air, and news is conveyed by television and newspapers)

VERBAL

MEGA: large, great

megalith: a very big stone

megalomania: a mental condition involving delusions of greatness; an obsession with doing great things

megalopolis: a very large city

megaphone: a device for magnifying the sound of one's voice

megaton: explosive power equal to 1,000 tons of T.N.T.

MICRO: very small

microbe: a very small organism

microcosm: a small system that reflects a larger whole

micron: a millionth of a meter

microorganism: a very small organism

microscope: a device that magnifies very small things for viewing

MIN: small

diminish: to lessen

diminution: the act or process of diminishing

miniature: a copy or model that represents something in greatly reduced size

minute: a unit of time equal to one-sixtieth of an hour

minutiae: small or trivial details

MIN: to project, to hang over

eminent: towering above others; projecting

imminent: about to occur; impending

preeminent: superior to or notable above all others

prominent: projecting outward

MIS: bad, wrong, to hate

misadventure: bad luck; an unlucky accident

misanthrope: one who hates people or humanity

misapply: to use something incorrectly

mischance: bad luck; an unlucky accident

mischief: bad or annoying behavior

misconstrue: to take something in a way that wasn't intended; to understand something incorrectly

misfit: somebody or something that doesn't fit in

MIS/MIT: to send

emissary: a messenger or agent sent to represent the interests of another

intermittent: stopping and starting at intervals

remission: a lessening of intensity or degree

remit: to send money

transmit: to send from one person, thing, or place to another

MISC: mixed

miscellaneous: made up of a variety of parts or ingredients

promiscuous: consisting of diverse and unrelated parts or individuals; indiscriminate

MOB/MOM/MOT/MOV: to move

automobile: a vehicle that moves under its own power; a motorized car

demote: to move downward in an organization

immovable: incapable of being moved; unyielding

locomotion: moving from place to place; the ability to do so

mob: the rabble; a disorderly group of people (from the Latin *mobile vulgus*, meaning "the fickle crowd")

mobile: movable

mobilize: to make ready for movement; to assemble

moment: an instant; importance

momentous: of great importance (originally: having the power to move)

momentum: the force driving a moving object to keep moving; a growing force

motion: movement

motive: a reason for action; what moves a person to do something

motor: a device that makes something move

mutiny: rebellion against authority, esp. by sailors

promote: to move to a higher rank in an organization

remove: to take away; to move away

MOLL: soft

emollient: something that softens or soothes (e.g., a lotion)

mild: gentle; kind

mollify: soothe; soften; calm

mollusk: a phylum of invertebrate animals—including octopuses, squids, oysters, clams, and slugs—with soft bodies

MON/MONO: one

monarchy: rule by a single person

monk: a man in a religious order living apart from society (originally: a religious hermit)

monochord: a musical instrument with a single string

monogram: a design combining multiple letters into one

monograph: a scholarly study of a single subject

VERBAL

monologue: a speech or other dramatic composition recited by one person

monomania: an obsession with a single subject

monotonous: boring; spoken using only one tone

MON/MONIT: to remind, to warn

admonish: to counsel against something; caution

monitor: one that admonishes, cautions, or reminds

monument: a structure, such as a building, tower, or sculpture, erected as a memorial

premonition: forewarning, presentiment

remonstrate: to say or plead in protect, objection, or reproof

summon: to call together; convene

MOR/MORT: death

immortal: not subject to death

morbid: susceptible to preoccupation with unwholesome matters

moribund: dying, decaying

MORPH: shape

amorphous: without definite form; lacking a specific shape

anthropomorphism: attribution of human characteristics to inanimate objects, animals, or natural phenomena

metamorphosis: a transformation, as by magic or sorcery

MULT: many

multiple: many, having many parts; a number containing some quantity of a smaller number without remainder

multiplex: having many parts; a movie theater or other building with many separate units

multiply: to increase; to become many

multitudinous: very many; containing very many; having very many forms

MUT: to change

commute: to substitute; exchange; interchange

immutable: unchangeable, invariable

mutation: the process of being changed

permutation: a complete change; transformation

transmute: to change from one form into another

NAT/NAS/NAI/GNA: birth

cognate: related by blood; having a common ancestor

naive: lacking worldliness and sophistication; artless

nascent: starting to develop

native: belonging to one by nature; inborn; innate

natural: present due to nature, not to artificial or man-made means

renaissance: rebirth, esp. referring to culture

NAU/NAV: ship, sailor

astronaut: one who travels in outer space

circumnavigate: to sail all the way around

cosmonaut: one who travels in outer space

nauseous: causing a squeamish feeling (originally: seasickness)

nautical: related to sailing or sailors

naval: related to the navy

nave: the central portion of a church (which resembles the shape of a ship)

navy: a military force consisting of ships and sailors

NIHIL: nothing, none

annihilate: wipe out; reduce to nothing

nihilism: denial of all moral beliefs; denial that existence has any meaning

NOC/NOX: harm

innocent: uncorrupted by evil, malice, or wrongdoing

innocuous: not harmful or injurious

noxious: injurious or harmful to health or morals

obnoxious: highly disagreeable or offensive

NOCT/NOX: night

equinox: one of two times in a year when day and night are equal in length

noctambulant: walking at night; sleepwalking

nocturnal: related to the night; active at night

nocturne: a dreamlike piece of music; a painting set at night

NOM: rule, order

astronomy: the scientific study of the universe beyond the Earth

autonomy: independence, self-governance

economy: the careful or thrifty use of resources, as of income, materials, or labor

gastronomy: the art or science of good eating

taxonomy: the science, laws, or principles of classification

NOM/NYM/NOUN/NOWN: name

acronym: a word formed from the initial letters of a name

anonymous: having an unknown or unacknowledged name

nomenclature: a system of names; systematic naming

nominal: existing in name only; negligible

nominate: to propose by name as a candidate

noun: a word that names a person, place, or thing

renown: fame; reputation

synonym: a word having a meaning similar to that of another word of the same language

NON: not

nonconformist: one who does not conform to a church or other societal institution

nonentity: something that doesn't exist; something that is unimportant

nonpareil: something with no equal

nonpartisan: not affiliated with a political party

NOUNC/NUNC: to announce

announce: to proclaim

pronounce: to articulate

renounce: to give up, especially by formal announcement

NOV/NEO/NOU: new

innovate: to begin or introduce something new

neologism: a newly coined word, phrase, or expression

neophyte: a beginner; a new convert; a new worker

neoplasm: a new growth in the body; a tumor

nouveau riche: one who has lately become rich

novice: a person new to any field or activity

renovate: to restore to an earlier condition

NULL: nothing

annul: to cancel; to make into nothing

nullify: to cancel; to make into nothing

nullity: the condition of being nothing

OB: toward, to, against, over

obese: extremely fat, corpulent

obfuscate: to render indistinct or dim; darken

oblique: having a slanting or sloping direction

obsequious: overly submissive

obstinate: stubbornly adhering to an idea, inflexible

obstreperous: noisily defiant, unruly

obstruct: to block or fill with obstacles

obtuse: not sharp, pointed, or acute in any form

OMNI: all

omnibus: an anthology of the works of one author or of writings on related subjects

omnipotent: all powerful

omnipresent: everywhere at one time

omniscient: having infinite knowledge

ONER: burden

exonerate: to free from blame (originally: to relieve of a burden)

onerous: burdensome; difficult

onus: a burden; a responsibility

OSS/OSTE: bone

ossify: to become bone; to harden; to become callous

ossuary: a place where bones are kept; a charnel house

osteopathy: a medical system based on the belief that many illnesses can be traced to issues in the skeletal system

PAC/PEAC: peace

appease: to bring peace to

pacifier: something or someone that eases the anger or agitation of

pacify: to ease the anger or agitation of

pact: a formal agreement, as between nations

PALP: to feel

palpable: capable of being felt; tangible

palpate: to feel; to examine by feeling

palpitate: to beat quickly, as the heart; to throb

PAN/PANT: all, everyone

pandemic: widespread, general, universal

panegyric: formal or elaborate praise at an assembly

panoply: a wide-ranging and impressive array or display

panorama: an unobstructed and wide view of an extensive area

pantheon: a public building containing tombs or memorials of the illustrious dead of a nation

PAR: equal

apartheid: any system or caste that separates people according to race, etc.

disparage: to belittle, speak disrespectfully about

disparate: essentially different

par: an equality in value or standing

parity: equally, as in amount, status, or character

PARA: next to, beside

parable: a short, allegorical story designed to illustrate a moral lesson or religious principle

paragon: a model of excellence

parallel: extending in the same direction

paranoid: suffering from a baseless distrust of others

parasite: an organism that lives on or within a plant or animal of another species, from which it obtains nutrients

parody: to imitate for purposes of satire

PAS/PAT/PATH: feeling, suffering, disease

compassion: a feeling of deep sympathy for someone struck by misfortune, accompanied by a desire to alleviate suffering

dispassionate: devoid of personal feeling or bias

empathy: the identification with the feelings or thoughts of others

impassive: showing or feeling no emotion

pathogenic: causing disease

sociopath: a person whose behavior is antisocial and who lacks a sense of moral responsibility

sympathy: harmony or agreement in feeling

PAU/PO/POV/PU: few, little, poor

impoverish: to deplete

paucity: smallness of quantity; scarcity; scantiness

pauper: a person without any personal means of support

poverty: the condition of being poor

puerile: childish, immature

pusillanimous: lacking courage or resolution

PEC: money

impecunious: having no money; penniless

peculation: embezzlement

pecuniary: relating to money

PED: child, education

encyclopedia: book or set of books containing articles on various topics, covering all branches of knowledge or of one particular subject

pedagogue: a teacher

pedant: one who displays learning ostentatiously

pediatrician: a doctor who primarily has children as patients

PED/POD: foot

antipodes: places that are diametrically opposite each other on the globe

expedite: to speed up the progress of

impede: to retard progress by means of obstacles or hindrances

pedal: a foot-operated lever or part used to control

pedestrian: a person who travels on foot

podium: a small platform for an orchestra conductor, speaker, etc.

PEL: to drive, to push

compel: to force; to command

dispel: to drive away; to disperse

expel: to drive out; to banish; to eject

impel: to force; to drive forward

propel: to drive forward

PEN/PUN: to pay, to compensate

penal: of or pertaining to punishment, as for crimes

penalty: a punishment imposed for a violation of law or rule

penance: a punishment undergone to express regret for a sin

penitent: contrite

punitive: serving for, concerned with, or inflicting punishment

PEN/PENE: almost

peninsula: a landmass that is mostly surrounded by water, making it almost an island

penultimate: second-to-last

penumbra: a shaded area between pure shadow and pure light

PEND/PENS: to hang, to weight, to pay

appendage: a limb or other subsidiary part that diverges from the central structure

appendix: supplementary material at the end of a text

compensate: to counterbalance, offset

depend: to rely; to place trust in

indispensable: absolutely necessary, essential, or requisite

stipend: a periodic payment; fixed or regular pay

PER: completely

perforate: to make a way through or into something

perfunctory: performed merely as routine duty

perplex: to cause to be puzzled or bewildered over what is not understood

VERBAL

VERBAL

persistent: lasting or enduring tenaciously

perspicacious: shrewd, astute

pertinacious: resolute, persistent

peruse: to read with thoroughness or care

PERI: around

perimeter: the border or outer boundary of a two-dimensional figure

peripatetic: walking or traveling about; itinerant

periscope: an optical instrument for seeing objects in an obstructed field of vision

PET/PIT: to go, to seek, to strive

appetite: a desire for food or drink

centripetal: moving toward the center

compete: to strive to outdo another

impetuous: characterized by sudden or rash action or emotion

petition: a formally drawn request soliciting some benefit

petulant: showing sudden irritation, esp. over some annoyance

PHIL: love

bibliophile: one who loves or collects books

philatelist: one who loves or collects postage stamps

philology: the study of literary texts to establish their authenticity and determine their meaning

philosophy: the rational investigation of the truths and principles of being, knowledge, or conduct

PHOB: fear

claustrophobia: fear of enclosed places

hydrophobia: fear of water, which is a symptom of rabies; rabies

phobia: fear; an irrational fear

xenophobia: fear of foreigners; hatred of foreigners

PHON: sound

euphony: the quality of sounding good

megaphone: a device for magnifying the sound of one's voice

phonetics: the study of the sounds used in speech

polyphony: the use of simultaneous melodic lines to produce harmonies in musical compositions

telephone: a device for transmitting sound at a distance

PHOTO: light

photograph: a picture, originally made by exposing chemically treated film to light

photon: a packet of light or other electromagnetic radiation

photosynthesis: a process by which plants create carbohydrates when under light

PLAC: to please

complacent: self-satisfied, unconcerned

complaisant: inclined or disposed to please

implacable: unable to be pleased

placebo: a substance with no pharmacological effect that acts to placate a patient who believes it to be a medicine

placid: pleasantly calm or peaceful

PLE/PLEN: to fill, full

complete: having all parts or elements

deplete: to decrease seriously or exhaust the supply of

implement: an instrument, tool, or utensil for accomplishing work

plethora: excess, overabundance

plenitude: fullness

replete: abundantly supplied

supplement: something added to supply a deficiency

PLEX/PLIC/PLY: to fold, twist, tangle, or bend

complex: composed of many interconnected parts

duplicity: deceitfulness in speech or conduct, double-dealing

implicate: to show to be involved, usually in an incriminating manner

implicit: not expressly stated, implied

replica: any close copy or reproduction

supplicate: to make humble and earnest entreaty

POLY: many

polyandry: the practice of having multiple husbands

polygamy: the practice of having multiple wives

polyglot: someone who speaks many languages

polygon: a figure with many sides

polytheism: belief in many gods

PON/POS/POUND: to put, to place

component: a constituent part, elemental ingredient

expose: to lay open to danger, attack, or harm

VERBAL

expound: to set forth in detail

juxtapose: to place close together or side by side

repository: a receptacle or place where things are deposited

PORT: to carry

deportment: conduct, behavior

disport: to divert or amuse oneself

export: to transmit abroad

import: to bring in from a foreign country

importune: to urge or press with excessive persistence

portable: easily carried

POST: behind, after

post facto: after the fact

posterior: situated at the rear

posterity: future generations

posthumous: after death

POT: to drink

potable: drinkable; safe to drink; a drink

potation: drinking; a drink

potion: a drinkable medicine, poison, or other concoction

PRE: before, in front

precarious: dependent on circumstances beyond one's control

precedent: an act that serves as an example for subsequent situations

precept: a commandment given as a rule of action or conduct

precocious: unusually advanced or mature in mental development or talent

premonition: a feeling of anticipation over a future event

presentiment: foreboding

PREHEND/PRISE: to take, to get, to seize

apprehend: to take into custody

comprise: to include or contain

enterprise: a project undertaken

reprehensible: deserving rebuke or censure

reprisals: retaliation against an enemy

surprise: to strike with an unexpected feeling of wonder or astonishment

PRI/PRIM: first

primary: first; most important

primal: original; most important

prime: first in quality; best

primeval: ancient; going back to the first age of the world

pristine: original; like new; unspoiled; pure

PRO: in front, before, much, for

problem: a difficult question (originally: one put before another for solution)

proceed: to go forward

VERBAL

profuse: spending or giving freely

prolific: highly fruitful

propound: to set forth for consideration

proselytize: to convert or attempt to recruit

provident: having or showing foresight

PROB: to prove, to test

approbation: praise, consideration

opprobrium: the disgrace incurred by shameful conduct

probe: to search or examine thoroughly

probity: honesty, high-mindedness

reprobate: a depraved or wicked person

PROP/PROX: near

approximate: very near; close to being accurate

proximate: nearby; coming just before or just after

proximity: nearness; distance

PROT/PROTO: first

protagonist: the main character in a play or story

protocol: diplomatic etiquette; a system of proper conduct; the original record of a treaty or other negotiation

prototype: the first version of an invention, on which later models are based

protozoan: belonging to a group of single-celled animals, which came before more complex animals

PSEUD/PSEUDO: false

pseudonym: a false name; a pen name

pseudopod: part of a single-celled organism that can be stuck out (like a foot) and used to move around

pseudoscience: false science; something believed to be based on the scientific method but that actually is not

PUG: to fight

impugn: to challenge as false

pugilist: a fighter or boxer

pugnacious: to quarrel or fight readily

repugnant: objectionable or offensive

PUNC/PUNG/POIGN: to point, to prick, to pierce

compunction: a feeling of uneasiness for doing wrong

expunge: to erase, eliminate completely

point: a sharp or tapering end

punctilious: strict or exact in the observance of formalities

VERBAL

VERBAL

puncture: the act of piercing

pungent: caustic or sharply
expressive

PYR: fire

pyre: a bonfire, usually for burning a dead body

pyromania: an urge to start fires

pyrosis: heartburn

pyrotechnics: fireworks

QUAD/QUAR/QUAT: four

quadrant: a quarter of a circle; a
90-degree arc

quadrille: a square dance involving four couples

quadruple: four times as many

quadruplets: four children born
in one birth

quart: one fourth of a gallon

quaternary: the number four;
the fourth in a series

QUE/QUIS: to seek

acquire: to come into possession of

conquest: the act gaining
control by force

exquisite: of special beauty or
charm

inquisitive: given to research,
eager for knowledge

perquisite: a gratuity, tip

querulous: full of complaints

query: a question, inquiry

QUIE/QUIT: quiet, rest

acquiesce: to comply, give in

disquiet: lack of calm or peace

quiescence: the condition of
being at rest, still, inactive

quiet: making little or no sound

tranquil: free from commotion
or tumult

QUIN/QUINT: five

quinquennial: a five-year period;
a fifth anniversary

quintessence: the essential part
of something (originally: the
"fifth essence," which was
believed to permeate everything and be what stars and
planets were made of)

quintuple: five times as many

RACI/RADI: root

deracinate: to uproot

eradicate: to uproot; to wipe
out

radical: pertaining to roots;
questioning everything, even
basic beliefs; going to root
causes; thorough

radish: a root vegetable

RAMI: branch

ramification: a branch; an
offshoot; a collection of
branches; a consequence

ramiform: branchlike

RE: back, again

recline: to lean back; to lie down

regain: to gain again; to take back

remain: to stay behind; to be left; to continue to be

reorganize: to organize again

request: to ask (originally: to seek again)

RECT: straight, right

correct: to set right

direct: to guide; to put straight

erect: upright; starting up straight

rectangle: a four-sided figure in which every angle is a right angle

rectitude: moral uprightness; moral straightness

REG: king, rule

interregnum: a period between kings

realm: a kingdom; a domain

regal: kingly; royal

regent: one who serves on behalf of a king; one who rules

regicide: killing a king; one who kills a king

regiment: a body of troops in an army; to form into such a body; to subject to strict rule

regular: having a structure following some rule; orderly; normally used; average

RETRO: backward

retroactive: extending to things that happened in the past

retrofit: to install newer parts into an older device or structure

retrograde: moving backward; appearing to move backward

retrospective: looking back at the past

RID/RIS: to laugh

derision: the act of mockery

risible: causing laughter

ROG: to ask

abrogate: to abolish by formal means

arrogant: making claims to superior importance or rights

arrogate: to claim unwarrantably or presumptuously

derogatory: belittling, disparaging

interrogate: to ask questions of, esp. formally

surrogate: a person appointed to act for another

RUB/RUD: red

rouge: a red powder used as makeup

rubella: German measles; a disease marked by red spots

rubicund: reddish; rosy-cheeked

VERBAL

rubric: a rule; a guide for scoring tests; a heading in a book set in red letters

russet: reddish-brown; a coarse cloth, usually reddish-brown; a type of apple or pear, typically reddish-brown

RUD: crude

erudite: scholarly; learned (that is, trained out of crudeness)

rude: uncivilized; impolite

rudimentary: undeveloped; related to rudiments

rudiments: first principles; imperfect first step of one's training

SACR/SANCT: holy

execrable: abominable

sacrament: something regarded as possessing sacred character

sacred: devoted or dedicated to a deity or religious purpose

sacrifice: the offering of some living or inanimate thing to a deity in homage

sacrilege: the violation of anything sacred

sanctify: to make holy

sanction: authoritative permission or approval

SAG/SAP/SAV: taste, thinking, discerning

insipid: tasteless

sagacious: perceptive; discerning; insightful

sage: wise

sapient: wise

savant: a learned person

savor: taste; to enjoy flavors

SAL/SIL/SAULT/SULT: to leap, to jump

assault: a sudden or violent attack

desultory: at random, unmethodical

exult: to show or feel triumphant joy

insolent: boldly rude or disrespectful

insult: to treat with contemptuous rudeness

resilient: able to spring back to an original form after compression

salient: prominent or conspicuous

somersault: to roll the body end over end, making a complete revolution

SAL: salt

salary: payment for services (originally: money for Roman soldiers to buy salt)

saline: containing salt; salty

SALU: health

salubrious: healthful

salutary: healthful

salute: to greet; a gesture of greeting (originally: to wish good health)

SALV: to save

salvage: to save; something saved or recovered

salvation: being saved

savior: one who saves

SAN: healthy

sane: mentally healthy

sanitarium: a place of healing

sanitary: promoting health; related to conditions that affect health, such as cleanliness

SANG: blood

consanguinity: being related by blood

sanguinary: bloody; bloodthirsty

sanguine: hopeful; confident (from the "sanguine humor," which was believed to be associated with those traits)

SAT: enough

assets: property; possessions (originally: enough property to cover one's debts)

dissatisfied: feeling that one does not have enough

sate: to fill

satisfy: to meet one's desires; to meet an obligation; to provide with enough

saturate: to fill completely; to entirely satisfy

SCI: to know

conscience: the inner sense of what is right or wrong, impelling one toward right action

conscious: aware of one's own existence

omniscient: knowing everything

prescient: having knowledge of things before they happen

unconscionable: unscrupulous

SCRIBE/SCRIPT: to write

ascribe: to credit or assign, as to a cause or course

circumscribe: to draw a line around

conscription: draft

describe: to tell or depict in words

postscript: any addition or supplement

proscribe: to condemn as harmful or odious

scribble: to write hastily or carelessly

script: handwriting

transcript: a written or typed copy

VERBAL

VERBAL

SE: apart, away

secede: to withdraw formally from an association

sedition: incitement of discontent or rebellion against a government

seduce: to lead astray

segregate: to separate or set apart from others

select: to choose in preference to another

separate: to keep apart, divide

sequester: to remove or withdraw into solitude or retirement

SEC/SEQU/SUE/SUI: to follow

non sequitur: an inference or a conclusion that does not follow from the premises

obsequious: fawning

prosecute: to seek to enforce by legal process

pursue: to chase after

second: next after the first

sequence: the following of one thing after another

suite: a series; a set (originally: a train of followers)

SED/SESS/SID: to sit, to settle

assiduous: diligent, persistent, hardworking (literally, "sitting down" to business)

dissident: disagreeing, as in opinion or attitude (literally, "sitting apart")

insidious: intended to entrap or beguile; lying in wait to entrap

preside: to exercise management or control; to sit in the leader's chair

resident: a person who lives in a place

residual: remaining, leftover

sediment: the matter that settles to the bottom of a liquid

session: a meeting at which people sit together in discussion

SEM: seed, to sow

disseminate: to spread; to scatter around

semen: seed (of male animals)

seminary: a school, esp. for religious training (originally: a place for raising plants)

SEMI: half

semicircle: half a circle

semiconscious: only partly conscious; half awake

SEN: old

senate: the highest legislative body (from "council of elders")

senescent: getting old

senile: relating to old age; experiencing memory loss or other age-related mental impairments

sire: a title for a king; a father
(originally: an important
person, an old man)

SENS/SENT: to feel, to be aware

dissent: to differ in opinion, esp.
from the majority

insensate: without feeling or
sensitivity

presentiment: a feeling that
something is about to
happen

resent: to feel or show displeasure

sense: any of the faculties by
which humans and animals
perceive stimuli originating
outside the body

sensory: of or pertaining to the
senses or sensation

sentiment: an attitude or feeling
toward something

sentinel: a person or thing that
stands watch

SIN/SINU: bend, fold, curve

insinuate: to introduce in
sneaky or winding ways

sinuous: moving in a bending
or wavy manner

sinus: a curved or irregularly
shaped cavity in the body,
such as those related to the
nostrils

SOL: alone

desolate: deserted; laid waste;
left alone

isolate: to set apart from others

soliloquize: talk to oneself; talk
onstage as if to oneself

solipsism: the belief that the
only thing that really exists,
or can really be known, is
oneself

solitude: the state of being
alone

SOL: to loosen, to free

absolution: forgiveness for
wrongdoing

dissolute: indifferent to moral
restraints

dissolution: the act or process
of dissolving into parts or
elements

dissolve: to make a solution of,
as by mixing in a liquid

resolution: a formal expression
of opinion or intention made

soluble: capable of being dis-
solved or liquefied

SOL: sun

parasol: an umbrella that pro-
tects from the sun

solar: related to the sun

solarium: a sunroom; a room
with windows for taking in
the sun

solstice: one of two days when
the sun reaches its highest

VERBAL

point at noon and seems to
stand still

SOMN: sleep

insomnia: inability to sleep
somnambulist: a sleepwalker
somniferous: sleep-inducing
somniloquist: one who talks
while asleep
somnolent: sleep-inducing;
sleepy; drowsy

SOPH: wisdom

philosopher: one who studies
logic, beauty, truth, etc.; one
who seeks wisdom
sophism: a superficially appeal-
ing but fallacious argument
sophisticated: complex; worldly;
experienced

SOURC/SURG/SURRECT: to rise

insurgent: rising up in revolution; rushing in
insurrection: rising up in armed
rebellion
resurrection: coming back to
life; rising again
source: where something comes
from (such as spring water
rising out of the ground)
surge: to rise up forcefully, as
ocean waves

SPEC/SPIC: to look, to see

circumspect: watchful and
discreet, cautious
conspicuous: easily seen or
noticed; readily observable
perspective: one's mental view
of facts, ideas, and their
interrelationships
perspicacious: having keen
mental perception and
understanding
retrospective: contemplative of
past situations
specious: deceptively attractive
spectrum: a broad range of
related things that form a
continuous series
speculation: the contemplation
or consideration of some
subject

SPIR: breath

aspire: to desire; to pant for
(originally: to breathe on)
expire: to breathe out; to
breathe one's last; to come
to an end
spirit: the breath of life; the soul;
an incorporeal supernatural
being; an outlook; a lively
quality

STA/STI: to stand, to be in place

apostasy: renunciation of an
object of one's previous
loyalty

constitute: to make up

destitute: without means of subsistence

obstinate: stubbornly adhering to a purpose, opinion, or course of action

stasis: the state of equilibrium or inactivity caused by opposing equal forces

static: of bodies or forces at rest or in equilibrium

STRICT/STRING/STRAN: to tighten, to bind

astringent: causing to tighten

constrain: to confine; to bind within certain limits

restriction: a limitation

strangle: to kill by suffocation, usually by tightening a cord or one's hand around the throat

SUA: sweet, pleasing, to urge

assuage: to make less severe, ease, relieve

dissuade: to deter; to advise against

persuade: to encourage; to convince

suave: smoothly agreeable or polite; sweet

SUB/SUP: below, under

subliminal: existing or operating below the threshold of confidence

submissive: inclined or ready to submit

subsidiary: serving to assist or supplement

subterfuge: an artifice or expedient used to evade a rule

subtle: thin, tenuous, or rarefied

suppose: to put down as a hypothesis; to use as the underlying basis of an argument; to assume

SUMM: highest, total

consummate: highly qualified; complete; perfect

sum: total; amount of money

summary: concise statement of the total findings on a subject; comprehensive

summit: highest point

SUPER/SUR: over, above

supercilious: arrogant, haughty, condescending

superfluous: extra, more than necessary

superlative: the highest kind or order

supersede: to replace in power, as by another person or thing

surmount: to get over or across, to prevail

surpass: to go beyond in amount, extent, or degree

surveillance: a watch kept over someone or something

VERBAL

VERBAL

SYM/SYN: together

symbiosis: living together in a mutually beneficial relationship

symmetry: balanced proportions; having opposite parts that mirror one another

sympathy: affinity; feeling affected by what happens to another

symposium: a meeting at which ideas are discussed (originally: a party at which people drink together)

synonym: a word that means the same thing as another

synthesis: combining things to create a new whole

TAC/TIC: to be silent

reticent: disposed to be silent or not to speak freely

tacit: unspoken understanding

taciturn: uncommunicative

TACT/TAG/TAM/TANG: to touch

contact: to touch; to get in touch

contagious: able to spread by contact, as disease

contaminate: to corrupt, taint, or otherwise damage the integrity of something by contact or mixture

contiguous: directly touching; sharing a boundary

intact: untouched; whole

intangible: unable to be touched

tactile: pertaining to touch; touchable

TAIN/TEN/TENT/TIN: to hold

abstention: the act of refraining voluntarily

detain: to keep from proceeding

pertain: to have reference or relation

pertinacious: persistent, stubborn

sustenance: nourishment, means of livelihood

tenable: capable of being held, maintained, or defended

tenacious: holding fast

tenure: the holding or possessing of anything

TEND/TENS/TENT/TENU: to stretch, to thin

attenuate: to weaken or reduce in force

contentious: quarrelsome, disagreeable, belligerent

distend: to expand by stretching

extenuating: making less serious by offering excuses

tendentious: having a predisposition toward a point of view

tension: the act of stretching or straining

tentative: of the nature of, or done as a trial, attempt

TEST: to bear witness

attest: bear witness

contest: to dispute (from bringing a lawsuit by calling witnesses)

detest: to despise; to hate (originally: to curse something by calling upon God to witness it)

protest: a dissent; a declaration, esp. of disagreement

testament: a statement of a person's wishes for the disposal of his or her property after death; a will

testify: bear witness

THEO: god

apotheosis: glorification, glorified ideal

atheist: one who does not believe in a deity or divine system

theocracy: a form of government in which a deity is recognized as the supreme ruler

theology: the study of divine things and the divine faith

THERM: heat

thermal: relating to heat; retaining heat

thermometer: a device for measuring heat

thermonuclear: relating to a nuclear reaction that takes place at high temperatures

thermostat: a device for regulating heat

TIM: fear

intimidate: to strike fear into; to make fearful

timid: fearful; shy

TOR/TORQ/TORT: to twist

contort: to twist; to distort

distort: to pull out of shape, often by twisting; to twist or misrepresent facts

extort: to wring money, property, or services out of somebody using threats or force

torch: a portable flame used for light (perhaps derived from hemp twisted around sticks, then dipped in pitch)

torque: twisting force; a force that creates rotation

tort: a wrongful act (other than breach of contract) that legally entitles one to damages

torture: to inflict pain (including by twisting instruments like the rack or wheel)

VERBAL

VERBAL

TORP: stiff, numb

torpedo: a explosive weapon used to sink ships (originally: a fish—the electric ray—that could shock victims to numbness)

torpid: numbed; sluggish

torpor: numbness; listlessness; apathy

TOX: poison

antitoxin: an antibody that counteracts a given poison

intoxication: being poisoned; drunkenness

toxic: poisonous

TRACT: to drag, to pull, to draw

abstract: to draw or pull away, remove

attract: to draw either by physical force or by an appeal to emotions or senses

contract: a legally binding document

detract: to take away from, esp. a positive thing

protract: to prolong, draw out, extend

tractable: easily managed or controlled

tractor: a powerful vehicle used to pull farm machinery

TRANS: across, beyond

intransigent: refusing to agree or compromise

transaction: the act of carrying on or conduct to a conclusion or settlement

transcendent: going beyond ordinary limits

transgress: to violate a law, command, or moral code

transition: a change from one way of being to another

transparent: easily seen through, recognized, or detected

ULT: last, beyond

penultimate: second-to-last

ulterior: beyond what is immediately present; future; beyond what is stated; hidden

ultimate: last; final

ultimatum: final offer; final terms

ultraviolet: beyond the violet end of the spectrum

UMBR: shadow

adumbrate: to foreshadow; to sketch; to overshadow

penumbra: a shaded area between pure shadow and pure light

somber: gloomy; darkened

umbrage: shade; shadow; displeasure; resentment

umbrella: a device providing shade from the sun or protection from rain

UN: not

unseen: not seen

unusual: not usual; exceptional; strange

UND: wave

abound: to be plentiful; to overflow (from water flowing in waves)

inundate: to flood

undulate: to move in a wavelike way

UNI/UN: one

reunion: a meeting that brings people back together

unanimous: of one mind; in complete accord

unicorn: a mythical animal with a single horn

uniform: of one kind; consistent

universe: all things considered as one whole

URB: city

suburb: a residential area just outside a city; an outlying area of a city

urban: relating to a city

urbane: polite; refined; polished (considered characteristic of those in cities)

urbanization: the process of an area becoming more like a city

US/UT: to use

abuse: to use wrongly or improperly

usage: a customary way of doing something

usurp: to seize and hold

utilitarian: efficient, functional, useful

VAIL/VAL: strength, use, worth

ambivalent: being caught between contradictory feelings of equal power or worth

avail: to have force; to be useful; to be of value

convalescent: recovering strength; healing

equivalent: of equal worth, strength, or use

evaluate: to determine the worth of

invalid: having no force or strength; void

valediction: a farewell (from wishing that someone be well; i.e., that someone have strength)

valid: having force; legally binding; effective; useful

value: worth

VERBAL

VERBAL

VEN/VENT: to come or to move toward

adventitious: accidental

contravene: to come into conflict with

convene: to assemble for some public purpose

intervene: to come between disputing factions, mediate

venturesome: showing a disposition to undertake risks

VER: truth

aver: to affirm, to declare to be true

veracious: habitually truthful

verdict: a judgment or decision

verisimilitude: the appearance or semblance of truth

verity: truthfulness

VERB: word

proverb: an adage; a byword; a short, commonly known saying

verbatim: exactly as stated; word-for-word

verbose: wordy

verbiage: excessive use of words; diction

VERD: green

verdant: green with vegetation; inexperienced

verdure: fresh, rich vegetation

VERS/VERT: to turn

aversion: dislike

avert: to turn away from

controversy: a public dispute involving a matter of opinion

diverse: of a different kind, form, character

extrovert: an outgoing person

inadvertent: unintentional

introvert: a person concerned primarily with inner thoughts and feelings

revert: to return to a former habit

VI: life

convivial: sociable

joie de vivre: joy of life (French expression)

viable: capable of living

vivacity: the quality of being lively, animated, spirited

vivid: strikingly bright or intense

VID/VIS: to see

adviser: one who gives counsel

evident: plain or clear to the sight or understanding

survey: to view in a general or comprehensive way

video: elements pertaining to the transmission or reception of an image

vista: a view or prospect

VIL: base, mean

revile: to criticize with harsh
  language
vile: loathsome, unpleasant
vilify: to slander, to defame

VIRU: poison

virulent: acrimonious; very bitter; very poisonous
viruliferous: containing a virus
virus: a submicroscopic agent
  that infects an organism and
  causes disease

VOC/VOK: call, word

advocate: to support or urge by
  argument
avocation: something one does
  in addition to a principle
  occupation
convoke: to call together
equivocate: to use ambiguous
  or unclear expressions
invoke: to call on a deity
vocabulary: the stock of words
  used by or known to a particular person or group
vocation: a particular occupation
vociferous: crying out noisily

VOL: wish

benevolent: characterized by or
  expressing goodwill
malevolent: characterized by or
  expressing bad will
volition: free choice, free will;
  act of choosing
voluntary: undertaken of one's
  own accord or by free choice

VOLU/VOLV: to roll, to turn

convolution: a twisting or
  folding
evolve: to develop naturally;
  literally, to unfold or unroll
revolt: to rebel; to turn against
  those in authority
revolve: to rotate; to turn
  around
voluble: easily turning; fluent;
  changeable
volume: a book (originally: a
  scroll); size or dimensions
  (originally: of a book)

VOR: to eat

carnivorous: meat-eating
omnivorous: eating or absorb-
  ing everything
voracious: having a great
  appetite

VERBAL

CHAPTER 3

Top GRE Words in Context

The GRE tests the same kinds of words over and over again. Here you will find some common GRE words with their definitions in context to help you to remember them. If you see a word that's unfamiliar to you, take a moment to study the definition and, most importantly, reread the sentence with the word's definition in mind.

Remember: Learning vocabulary words in context is one of the best ways for your brain to retain the words' meanings. A broader vocabulary will serve you well on all four GRE Verbal question types and will also be extremely helpful in the Analytical Writing section.

ABATE: to reduce in amount, degree, or severity

As the hurricane's force ABATED, the winds dropped and the sea became calm.

ABSCOND: to leave secretly

The patron ABSCONDED from the restaurant without paying his bill by sneaking out the back door.

ABSTAIN: to choose not to do something

She ABSTAINED from choosing a mouthwatering dessert from the tray.

ABYSS: an extremely deep hole

The submarine dove into the ABYSS to chart the previously unseen depths.

ADULTERATE: to make impure

The chef made his ketchup last longer by ADULTERATING it with water.

ADVOCATE: to speak in favor of

The vegetarian ADVOCATED a diet containing no meat.

AESTHETIC: concerning the appreciation of beauty

Followers of the AESTHETIC Movement regarded the pursuit of beauty as the only true purpose of art.

AGGRANDIZE: to increase in power, influence, and reputation

The supervisor sought to AGGRANDIZE herself by claiming that the achievements of her staff were actually her own.

ALLEVIATE: to make more bearable

Taking aspirin helps to ALLEVIATE a headache.

VERBAL

AMALGAMATE: to combine; to mix together

Giant Industries AMALGAMATED with Mega Products to form Giant-Mega Products Incorporated.

AMBIGUOUS: doubtful or uncertain; able to be interpreted several ways

The directions she gave were so AMBIGUOUS that we disagreed on which way to turn.

AMELIORATE: to make better; to improve

The doctor was able to AMELIORATE the patient's suffering using painkillers.

ANACHRONISM: something out of place in time

The aged hippie used ANACHRONISTIC phrases like *groovy* and *far out* that had not been popular for years.

ANALOGOUS: similar or alike in some way; equivalent to

In the Newtonian construct for explaining the existence of God, the universe is ANALOGOUS to a mechanical timepiece, the creation of a divinely intelligent "clockmaker."

ANOMALY: deviation from what is normal

Albino animals may display too great an ANOMALY in their coloring to attract normally colored mates.

ANTAGONIZE: to annoy or provoke to anger

The child discovered that he could ANTAGONIZE the cat by pulling its tail.

ANTIPATHY: extreme dislike

The ANTIPATHY between the French and the English regularly erupted into open warfare.

APATHY: lack of interest or emotion

The APATHY of voters is so great that less than half the people who are eligible to vote actually bother to do so.

ARBITRATE: to judge a dispute between two opposing parties

Since the couple could not come to agreement, a judge was forced to ARBITRATE their divorce proceedings.

ARCHAIC: ancient, old-fashioned

Her ARCHAIC Commodore computer could not run the latest software.

ARDOR: intense and passionate feeling

Bishop's ARDOR for the landscape was evident when he passionately described the beauty of the scenic Hudson Valley.

ARTICULATE: able to speak clearly and expressively

She is such an ARTICULATE defender of labor that unions are among her strongest supporters.

ASSUAGE: to make something unpleasant less severe

Serena used aspirin to ASSUAGE her pounding headache.

ATTENUATE: to reduce in force or degree; to weaken

The Bill of Rights ATTENUATED the traditional power of governments to change laws at will.

AUDACIOUS: fearless and daring

Her AUDACIOUS nature allowed her to fulfill her dream of skydiving.

AUSTERE: severe or stern in appearance; undecorated

The lack of decoration makes military barracks seem AUSTERE to the civilian eye.

VERBAL

BANAL: predictable, clichéd, boring

He used BANAL phrases like *Have a nice day*, or *Another day, another dollar.*

BOLSTER: to support; to prop up

The presence of giant footprints BOLSTERED the argument that Sasquatch was in the area.

BOMBASTIC: pompous in speech and manner

The ranting of the radio talk-show host was mostly BOMBASTIC; his boasting and outrageous claims had no basis in fact.

CACOPHONY: harsh, jarring noise

The junior high orchestra created an almost unbearable CACOPHONY as they tried to tune their instruments.

CANDID: impartial and honest in speech

The observations of a child can be charming since they are CANDID and unpretentious.

CAPRICIOUS: changing one's mind quickly and often

Queen Elizabeth I was quite CAPRICIOUS; her courtiers could never be sure which of their number would catch her fancy.

CASTIGATE: to punish or criticize harshly

Many Americans are amazed at how harshly the authorities in Singapore CASTIGATE perpetrators of what would be considered minor crimes in the United States.

CATALYST: something that brings about a change in something else

The imposition of harsh taxes was the CATALYST that finally brought on the revolution.

VERBAL

CAUSTIC: biting in wit

Dorothy Parker gained her reputation for CAUSTIC wit from her cutting, yet clever, insults.

CHAOS: great disorder or confusion

In many religious traditions, God created an ordered universe from CHAOS.

CHAUVINIST: someone prejudiced in favor of a group to which he or she belongs

The attitude that men are inherently superior to women and therefore must be obeyed is common among male CHAUVINISTS.

CHICANERY: deception by means of craft or guile

Dishonest used car sales people often use CHICANERY to sell their beat-up old cars.

COGENT: convincing and well reasoned

Swayed by the COGENT argument of the defense, the jury had no choice but to acquit the defendant.

CONDONE: to overlook, pardon, or disregard

Some theorists believe that failing to prosecute minor crimes is the same as CONDONING an air of lawlessness.

CONVOLUTED: intricate and complicated

Although many people bought *A Brief History of Time*, few could follow its CONVOLUTED ideas and theories.

CORROBORATE: to provide supporting evidence

Fingerprints CORROBORATED the witness's testimony that he saw the defendant in the victim's apartment.

CREDULOUS: too trusting; gullible

Although some four-year-olds believe in the Easter Bunny, only the most CREDULOUS nine-year-olds also believe in him.

CRESCENDO: steadily increasing volume or force

The CRESCENDO of tension became unbearable as Evel Knievel prepared to jump his motorcycle over the school buses.

DECORUM: appropriateness of behavior or conduct; propriety

The countess complained that the vulgar peasants lacked the DECORUM appropriate for a visit to the palace.

DEFERENCE: respect, courtesy

The respectful young law clerk treated the Supreme Court justice with the utmost DEFERENCE.

DERIDE: to speak of or treat with contempt; to mock

The awkward child was often DERIDED by his "cooler" peers.

DESICCATE: to dry out thoroughly

After a few weeks of lying on the desert's baking sands, the cow's carcass became completely DESICCATED.

DESULTORY: jumping from one thing to another; disconnected

Diane had a DESULTORY academic record; she had changed majors 12 times in three years.

DIATRIBE: an abusive, condemnatory speech

The trucker bellowed a DIATRIBE at the driver who had cut him off.

DIFFIDENT: lacking self-confidence

Steve's DIFFIDENT manner during the job interview stemmed from his nervous nature and lack of experience in the field.

VERBAL

VERBAL

DILATE: to make larger; to expand

When you enter a darkened room, the pupils of your eyes DILATE to let in more light.

DILATORY: intended to delay

The congressman used DILATORY measures to delay the passage of the bill.

DILETTANTE: someone with an amateurish and superficial interest in a topic

Jerry's friends were such DILETTANTES that they seemed to have new jobs and hobbies every week.

DIRGE: a funeral hymn or mournful speech

Melville wrote the poem "A DIRGE for James McPherson" for the funeral of a Union general who was killed in 1864.

DISABUSE: to set right; to free from error

Galileo's observations DISABUSED scholars of the notion that the sun revolved around the earth.

DISCERN: to perceive; to recognize

It is easy to DISCERN the difference between butter and butter-flavored topping.

DISPARATE: fundamentally different; entirely unlike

Although the twins appear to be identical physically, their personalities are DISPARATE.

DISSEMBLE: to present a false appearance; to disguise one's real intentions or character

The villain could DISSEMBLE to the police no longer—he admitted the deed and tore up the floor to reveal the body of the old man.

DISSONANCE: a harsh and disagreeable combination, often of sounds

Cognitive DISSONANCE is the inner conflict produced when long-standing beliefs are contradicted by new evidence.

DOGMA: a firmly held opinion, often a religious belief

Linus's central DOGMA was that children who believed in the Great Pumpkin would be rewarded.

DOGMATIC: dictatorial in one's opinions

The dictator was DOGMATIC—he, and only he, was right.

DUPE: to deceive; a person who is easily deceived

Bugs Bunny was able to DUPE Elmer Fudd by dressing up as a lady rabbit.

ECLECTIC: selecting from or made up from a variety of sources

Budapest's architecture is an ECLECTIC mix of Eastern and Western styles.

EFFICACY: effectiveness

The EFFICACY of penicillin was unsurpassed when it was first introduced; the drug completely eliminated almost all bacterial infections for which it was administered.

ELEGY: a sorrowful poem or speech

Although Thomas Gray's "ELEGY Written in a Country Churchyard" is about death and loss, it urges its readers to endure this life and to trust in spirituality.

ELOQUENT: persuasive and moving, especially in speech

The Gettysburg Address is moving not only because of its lofty sentiments but also because of its ELOQUENT words.

VERBAL

EMULATE: to copy; to try to equal or excel

The graduate student sought to EMULATE his professor in every way, copying not only how she taught but also how she conducted herself outside of class.

ENERVATE: to reduce in strength

The guerrillas hoped that a series of surprise attacks would ENERVATE the regular army.

ENGENDER: to produce, cause, or bring about

His fear and hatred of clowns was ENGENDERED when he witnessed the death of his father at the hands of a clown.

ENIGMA: a puzzle; a mystery

Speaking in riddles and dressed in old robes, the artist gained a reputation as something of an ENIGMA.

ENUMERATE: to count, list, or itemize

Moses returned from the mountain with tablets on which the commandments were ENUMERATED.

EPHEMERAL: lasting a short time

The lives of mayflies seem EPHEMERAL to us, since the flies' average life span is a matter of hours.

EQUIVOCATE: to use expressions of double meaning in order to mislead

When faced with criticism of her policies, the politician EQUIVOCATED and left all parties thinking she agreed with them.

ERRATIC: wandering and unpredictable

The plot seemed predictable until it suddenly took a series of ERRATIC turns that surprised the audience.

VERBAL

ERUDITE: learned, scholarly, bookish

The annual meeting of philosophy professors was a gathering of the most ERUDITE, well-published individuals in the field.

ESOTERIC: known or understood by only a few

Only a handful of experts are knowledgeable about the ESOTERIC world of particle physics.

ESTIMABLE: admirable

Most people consider it ESTIMABLE that Mother Teresa spent her life helping the poor of India.

EULOGY: speech in praise of someone

His best friend gave the EULOGY, outlining his many achievements and talents.

EUPHEMISM: use of an inoffensive word or phrase in place of a more distasteful one

The funeral director preferred to use the EUPHEMISM *sleeping* instead of the word *dead*.

EXACERBATE: to make worse

It is unwise to take aspirin to try to relieve heartburn; instead of providing relief, the drug will only EXACERBATE the problem.

EXCULPATE: to clear from blame; prove innocent

The adversarial legal system is intended to convict those who are guilty and to EXCULPATE those who are innocent.

EXIGENT: urgent; requiring immediate action

The patient was losing blood so rapidly that it was EXIGENT to stop the source of the bleeding.

VERBAL

VERBAL

EXONERATE: to clear of blame

The fugitive was EXONERATED when another criminal confessed to committing the crime.

EXPLICIT: clearly stated or shown; forthright in expression

The owners of the house left a list of EXPLICIT instructions detailing their house-sitter's duties, including a schedule for watering the house plants.

FANATICAL: acting excessively enthusiastic; filled with extreme, unquestioned devotion

The stormtroopers were FANATICAL in their devotion to the emperor, readily sacrificing their lives for him.

FAWN: to grovel

The understudy FAWNED over the director in hopes of being cast in the part on a permanent basis.

FERVID: intensely emotional; feverish

The fans of Maria Callas were unusually FERVID, doing anything to catch a glimpse of the great opera singer.

FLORID: excessively decorated or embellished

The palace had been decorated in a FLORID style; every surface had been carved and gilded.

FOMENT: to arouse or incite

The protesters tried to FOMENT feeling against the war through their speeches and demonstrations.

FRUGALITY: a tendency to be thrifty or cheap

Scrooge McDuck's FRUGALITY was so great that he accumulated enough wealth to fill a giant storehouse with money.

GARRULOUS: tending to talk a lot

The GARRULOUS parakeet distracted its owner with its continuous talking.

GREGARIOUS: outgoing, sociable

She was so GREGARIOUS that when she found herself alone, she felt quite sad.

GUILE: deceit or trickery

Since he was not fast enough to catch the roadrunner on foot, the coyote resorted to GUILE in an effort to trap his enemy.

GULLIBLE: easily deceived

The con man pretended to be a bank officer so as to fool GULLIBLE bank customers into giving him their account information.

HOMOGENOUS: of a similar kind

The class was fairly HOMOGENOUS, since almost all of the students were senior journalism majors.

ICONOCLAST: one who opposes established beliefs, customs, and institutions

His lack of regard for traditional beliefs soon established him as an ICONOCLAST.

IMPERTURBABLE: not capable of being disturbed

The counselor had so much experience dealing with distraught children that she seemed IMPERTURBABLE, even when faced with the wildest tantrums.

IMPERVIOUS: impossible to penetrate; incapable of being affected

A good raincoat will be IMPERVIOUS to moisture.

VERBAL

VERBAL

IMPETUOUS: quick to act without thinking

It is not good for an investment broker to be IMPETUOUS, since much thought should be given to all the possible options.

IMPLACABLE: unable to be calmed down or made peaceful

His rage at the betrayal was so great that he remained IMPLACABLE for weeks.

INCHOATE: not fully formed; disorganized

The ideas expressed in Nietzsche's mature work also appear in an INCHOATE form in his earliest writing.

INGENUOUS: showing innocence or childlike simplicity

She was so INGENUOUS that her friends feared that her innocence and trustfulness would be exploited when she visited the big city.

INIMICAL: hostile, unfriendly

Even though the children had grown up together, they were INIMICAL to each other at school.

INNOCUOUS: harmless

Some snakes are poisonous, but most species are INNOCUOUS and pose no danger to humans.

INSIPID: lacking interest or flavor

The critic claimed that the painting was INSIPID, containing no interesting qualities at all.

INTRANSIGENT: uncompromising; refusing to be reconciled

The professor was INTRANSIGENT on the deadline, insisting that everyone turn the assignment in at the same time.

INUNDATE: to overwhelm; to cover with water

The tidal wave INUNDATED Atlantis, which was lost beneath the water.

IRASCIBLE: easily made angry

Attila the Hun's IRASCIBLE and violent nature made all who dealt with him fear for their lives.

LACONIC: using few words

She was a LACONIC poet who built her reputation on using words as sparingly as possible.

LAMENT: to express sorrow; to grieve

The children continued to LAMENT the death of the goldfish weeks after its demise.

LAUD: to give praise; to glorify

Parades and fireworks were staged to LAUD the success of the rebels.

LAVISH: to give unsparingly (v.); extremely generous or extravagant (adj.)

She LAVISHED the puppy with so many treats that it soon became overweight and spoiled.

LETHARGIC: acting in an indifferent or slow, sluggish manner

The clerk was so LETHARGIC that, even when the store was slow, he always had a long line in front of him.

LOQUACIOUS: talkative

She was naturally LOQUACIOUS, which was a problem in situations in which listening was more important than talking.

VERBAL

LUCID: clear and easily understood

The explanations were written in a simple and LUCID manner so that students were immediately able to apply what they learned.

LUMINOUS: bright, brilliant, glowing

The park was bathed in LUMINOUS sunshine, which warmed the bodies and the souls of the visitors.

MALINGER: to evade responsibility by pretending to be ill

A common way to avoid the draft was by MALINGERING—pretending to be mentally or physically ill so as to avoid being taken by the Army.

MALLEABLE: capable of being shaped

Gold is the most MALLEABLE of precious metals; it can easily be formed into almost any shape.

METAPHOR: a figure of speech comparing two different things; a symbol

The METAPHOR "a sea of troubles" suggests a lot of troubles by comparing their number to the vastness of the sea.

METICULOUS: extremely careful about details

To find all the clues at the crime scene, the investigators METICULOUSLY examined every inch of the area.

MISANTHROPE: a person who dislikes others

The character Scrooge in *A Christmas Carol* is such a MISANTHROPE that even the sight of children singing makes him angry.

MITIGATE: to soften; to lessen

A judge may MITIGATE a sentence if she decides that a person committed a crime out of need.

MOLLIFY: to calm or make less severe

Their argument was so intense that it was difficult to believe any compromise would MOLLIFY them.

MONOTONY: lack of variation

The MONOTONY of the sound of the dripping faucet almost drove the research assistant crazy.

NAIVE: lacking sophistication or experience

Having never traveled before, the elementary school students were more NAIVE than their high school counterparts on the field trip.

OBDURATE: hardened in feeling; resistant to persuasion

The president was completely OBDURATE on the issue, and no amount of persuasion would change his mind.

OBSEQUIOUS: overly submissive and eager to please

The OBSEQUIOUS new associate made sure to compliment her supervisor's tie and agree with him on every issue.

OBSTINATE: stubborn, unyielding

The OBSTINATE child could not be made to eat any food that he disliked.

OBVIATE: to prevent; to make unnecessary

The river was shallow enough to wade across at many points, which OBVIATED the need for a bridge.

OCCLUDE: to stop up; to prevent the passage of

A shadow is thrown across the earth's surface during a solar eclipse, when the light from the sun is OCCLUDED by the moon.

ONEROUS: troublesome and oppressive; burdensome
The assignment was so extensive and difficult to manage that it proved ONEROUS to the team in charge of it.

OPAQUE: impossible to see through; preventing the passage of light
The heavy buildup of dirt and grime on the windows almost made them OPAQUE.

OPPROBRIUM: public disgrace
After the scheme to embezzle the elderly was made public, the treasurer resigned in utter OPPROBRIUM.

OSTENTATION: excessive showiness
The OSTENTATION of the Sun King's court is evident in the lavish decoration and luxuriousness of his palace at Versailles.

PARADOX: a contradiction or dilemma
It is a PARADOX that those most in need of medical attention are often those least able to obtain it.

PARAGON: model of excellence or perfection
She is the PARAGON of what a judge should be: honest, intelligent, hardworking, and just.

PEDANT: someone who shows off learning
The graduate instructor's tedious and excessive commentary on the subject soon gained her a reputation as a PEDANT.

PERFIDIOUS: willing to betray one's trust
The actress's PERFIDIOUS companion revealed all of her intimate secrets to the gossip columnist.

VERBAL

PERFUNCTORY: done in a routine way; indifferent

The machinelike bank teller processed the transaction and gave the waiting customer a PERFUNCTORY smile.

PERMEATE: to penetrate

This miraculous new cleaning fluid is able to PERMEATE stains and dissolve them in minutes!

PHILANTHROPY: charity; a desire or effort to promote goodness

New York's Metropolitan Museum of Art owes much of its collection to the PHILANTHROPY of private collectors who willed their estates to the museum.

PLACATE: to soothe or pacify

The burglar tried to PLACATE the snarling dog by saying "Nice doggy," and offering it a treat.

PLASTIC: able to be molded, altered, or bent

The new material was very PLASTIC and could be formed into products of vastly different shapes.

PLETHORA: excess

Assuming that more was better, the defendant offered the judge a PLETHORA of excuses.

PRAGMATIC: practical as opposed to idealistic

While daydreaming gamblers think they can get rich by frequenting casinos, PRAGMATIC gamblers realize that the odds are heavily stacked against them.

PRECIPITATE: to throw violently or bring about abruptly; lacking deliberation

Upon learning that the couple married after knowing each other only two months, friends and family members expected such a PRECIPITATE marriage to end in divorce.

VERBAL

PREVARICATE: to lie or deviate from the truth

Rather than admit that he had overslept again, the employee PREVARICATED and claimed that heavy traffic had prevented him from arriving at work on time.

PRISTINE: fresh and clean; uncorrupted

Since concerted measures had been taken to prevent looting, the archeological site was still PRISTINE when researchers arrived.

PRODIGAL: lavish, wasteful

The PRODIGAL son quickly wasted all of his inheritance on a lavish lifestyle devoted to pleasure.

PROLIFERATE: to increase in number quickly

Although she only kept two guinea pigs initially, they PROLIFERATED to such an extent that she soon had dozens.

PROPITIATE: to conciliate; to appease

The management PROPITIATED the irate union by agreeing to raise wages for its members.

PROPRIETY: correct behavior; obedience to rules and customs

The aristocracy maintained a high level of PROPRIETY, adhering to even the most minor social rules.

PRUDENCE: wisdom, caution, or restraint

The college student exhibited PRUDENCE by obtaining practical experience along with her studies, which greatly strengthened her résumé.

PUNGENT: sharp and irritating to the senses

The smoke from the burning tires was extremely PUNGENT.

VERBAL

QUIESCENT: motionless

Many animals are QUIESCENT over the winter months, minimizing activity in order to conserve energy.

RAREFY: to make thinner or sparser

Since the atmosphere RAREFIES as altitudes increase, the air at the top of very tall mountains is too thin to breathe.

REPUDIATE: to reject the validity of

The old woman's claim that she was Russian royalty was REPUDIATED when DNA tests showed she was of no relation to them.

RETICENT: silent, reserved

Physically small and RETICENT In her speech, Joan Didion often went unnoticed by those upon whom she was reporting.

RHETORIC: effective writing or speaking

Lincoln's talent for RHETORIC was evident in his beautifully expressed Gettysburg Address.

SATIATE: to satisfy fully or overindulge

His desire for power was so great that nothing less than complete control of the country could SATIATE it.

SOPORIFIC: causing sleep or lethargy

The movie proved to be so SOPORIFIC that soon loud snores were heard throughout the theater.

SPECIOUS: deceptively attractive; seemingly plausible but fallacious

The student's SPECIOUS excuse for being late sounded legitimate but was proved otherwise when her teacher called her home.

VERBAL

STIGMA: a mark of shame or discredit

In *The Scarlet Letter*, Hester Prynne was required to wear the letter *A* on her clothes as a public STIGMA for her adultery.

STOLID: unemotional; lacking sensitivity

The prisoner appeared STOLID and unaffected by the judge's harsh sentence.

SUBLIME: lofty or grand

The music was so SUBLIME that it transformed the rude surroundings into a special place.

TACIT: done without using words

Although not a word had been said, everyone in the room knew that a TACIT agreement had been made about which course of action to take.

TACITURN: silent, not talkative

The clerk's TACITURN nature earned him the nickname "Silent Bob."

TIRADE: long, harsh speech or verbal attack

Observers were shocked at the manager's TIRADE over such a minor mistake.

TORPOR: extreme mental and physical sluggishness

After surgery, the patient experienced TORPOR until the anesthesia wore off.

TRANSITORY: temporary, lasting a brief time

The reporter lived a TRANSITORY life, staying in one place only long enough to cover the current story.

VACILLATE: to sway physically; to be indecisive

The customer held up the line as he VACILLATED between ordering chocolate chip or rocky road ice cream.

VERBAL

VENERATE: to respect deeply

In a traditional Confucian society, the young VENERATE their elders, deferring to the elders' wisdom and experience.

VERACITY: filled with truth and accuracy

She had a reputation for VERACITY, so everyone trusted her description of events.

VERBOSE: wordy

The professor's answer was so VERBOSE that his student forgot what the original question had been.

VEX: to annoy

The old man who loved his peace and quiet was VEXED by his neighbor's loud music.

VOLATILE: easily aroused or changeable; lively or explosive

His VOLATILE personality made it difficult to predict his reaction to anything.

WAVER: to fluctuate between choices

If you WAVER too long before making a decision about which testing site to register for, you may not get your first choice.

WHIMSICAL: acting in a fanciful or capricious manner; unpredictable

The ballet was WHIMSICAL, delighting the children with its imaginative characters and unpredictable sets.

ZEAL: passion, excitement

She brought her typical ZEAL to the project, sparking enthusiasm in the other team members.

VERBAL

COMMONLY CONFUSED WORDS

Already—by this or that time, previously
He already completed his work.
All ready—completely prepared
The students were all ready to take their exam.

Altogether—entirely, completely
I am altogether certain that I turned in my homework.
All together—in the same place
She kept the figurines all together on her mantle.

Capital—a city containing the seat of government, the wealth or funds owned by a business or individual, resources
Atlanta is the capital of Georgia.
The company's capital gains have diminished in recent years.
Capitol—the building in which a legislative body meets
Our trip included a visit to the Capitol building in Washington, D.C.

Coarse—rough, not smooth; lacking refinement
The truck's large wheels enabled it to navigate the coarse, rough terrain.
His coarse language prevented him from getting hired for the job.
Course—path, series of classes or studies
James's favorite course is biology.
The doctor suggested that Amy rest and let the disease run its course.

Here—in this location
George Washington used to live here.
Hear—to listen to or to perceive by the ear
Did you hear the question?

Its—a personal pronoun that shows possession
Please put the book back in its place.
It's—the contraction of "it is" or "it has"
It's snowing outside.
It's been too long.

Lead—to act as a leader, to go first, or to take a superior position
The guide will lead us through the forest.
Led—past tense of "lead"
The guide led us through the forest.
Lead—a metal
It is dangerous to inhale fumes from paint containing lead.

Loose—free, to set free, not tight
She always wears loose clothing when she does yoga.
Lose—to become without
Use a bookmark so you don't lose your place in your book.

Passed—the past tense of pass, a euphemism for someone dying
We passed by her house on Sunday.
Past—that which has gone by or elapsed in time
In the past, Abby never used to study.
We drove past her house.

Principal—the head of a school, main or important
The quarterback's injury is the principal reason the team lost.
The principal of the school meets with parents regularly.
Principle—a fundamental law or truth
The laws of motion are among the most important principles in physics.

Stationary—fixed, not moving
Thomas rode a stationary bicycle at the gym.
Stationery—paper used for letter writing
The principal's stationery has the school's logo on the top.

Their—possessive of "they"
Paul and Ben studied for their test together.
There—a place, in that matter or respect
There are several question types on the GRE.
Please hang up your jacket over there.
They're—contraction of "they are"
Be careful of the bushes as they're filled with thorns.

VERBAL

PART TWO

Math Reference

CHAPTER 4

Top 100 GRE Math Concepts

The math on the GRE covers a lot of ground—from number properties and arithmetic to basic algebra and symbol problems to geometry and statistics. Don't let yourself be intimidated.

We've highlighted the 100 most important concepts that you need to know and divided them into three levels. The GRE Quantitative sections test your understanding of a relatively limited number of mathematical concepts, all of which you will be able to master.

Level 1 consists of foundational math topics. Though these topics may seem basic, review this list so that you are aware that these skills may play a part in the questions you will answer on the GRE. Look over the Level 1 list to make sure you're comfortable with the basics.

Level 2 is where most people start their review of math. Level 2 skills and formulas come into play quite frequently on the GRE. If the skills needed to handle Level 1 or 2 topics are keeping you from feeling up to the tasks expected on the GRE Quantitative section, you might consider taking the Kaplan GRE Math Refresher course.

Level 3 represents the most challenging math concepts you'll find on the GRE. Don't spend a lot of time on Level 3 if you still have gaps in Level 2, but once you've mastered Level 2, tackling Level 3 can put you over the top.

LEVEL 1

1. How to add, subtract, multiply, and divide WHOLE NUMBERS

You can check addition with subtraction.

$$17 + 5 = 22 \qquad 22 - 5 = 17$$

You can check multiplication with division.

$$5 \times 28 = 140 \qquad 140 \div 5 = 28$$

2. How to add, subtract, multiply, and divide FRACTIONS

Find a common denominator before adding or subtracting fractions.

$$\frac{4}{5} + \frac{3}{10} = \frac{8}{10} + \frac{3}{10} = \frac{11}{10} \text{ or } 1\frac{1}{10}$$

$$2 - \frac{3}{8} = \frac{16}{8} - \frac{3}{8} = \frac{13}{8} \text{ or } 1\frac{5}{8}$$

To multiply fractions, multiply the numerators first and then multiply the denominators. Simplify if necessary.

$$\frac{3}{4} \times \frac{1}{6} = \frac{3}{24} = \frac{1}{8}$$

You can also reduce before multiplying numerators and denominators. This keeps the products small.

$$\frac{5}{8} \times \frac{2}{15} = \frac{\overset{1}{5}}{\underset{4}{8}} \times \frac{\overset{1}{2}}{\underset{3}{15}} = \frac{1}{12}$$

To divide by a fraction, multiply by its reciprocal. To write the reciprocal of a fraction, flip the numerator and the denominator.

$$5 \div \frac{1}{3} = \frac{5}{1} \times \frac{3}{1} = 15 \qquad \frac{1}{3} \div \frac{4}{5} = \frac{1}{3} \times \frac{5}{4} = \frac{5}{12}$$

MATH

3. How to add, subtract, multiply, and divide DECIMALS

To add or subtract, align the decimal points and then add or subtract normally. Place the decimal point in the answer directly below existing decimal points.

$$\begin{array}{r} 3.25 \\ + 4.4 \\ \hline 7.65 \end{array} \qquad \begin{array}{r} 7.65 \\ - 4.4 \\ \hline 3.25 \end{array}$$

To multiply with decimals, multiply the digits normally and count off decimal places (equal to the total number of places in the factors) from the right.

$$2.5 \times 2.5 = 6.25$$
$$0.06 \times 2,000 = 120.00 = 120$$

To divide by a decimal, move the decimal point in the divisor to the right to form a whole number; move the decimal point in the dividend the same number of places. Divide as though there were no decimals, then place the decimal point in the quotient.

$$6.25 \div 2.5$$
$$= 62.5 \div 25 = 2.5$$

4. How to convert FRACTIONS TO DECIMALS and DECIMALS TO FRACTIONS

To convert a fraction to a decimal, divide the numerator by the denominator.

$$\frac{4}{5} = 0.8 \qquad \frac{4}{50} = 0.08 \qquad \frac{4}{500} = 0.008$$

To convert a decimal to a fraction, write the digits in the numerator and use the decimal name in the denominator.

$$0.003 = \frac{3}{1,000} \quad 0.03 = \frac{3}{100} \quad 0.3 = \frac{3}{10}$$

5. How to add, subtract, multiply, and divide POSITIVE AND NEGATIVE NUMBERS

When addends (the numbers being added) have the same sign, add their absolute values; the sum has the same sign as the addends. But when addends have different signs, subtract the absolute values; the sum has the sign of the greater absolute value.

$3 + 9 = 12$, but $-3 + (-9) = -12$
$3 + (-9) = -6$, but $-3 + 9 = 6$

In multiplication and division, when the signs are the same, the product/quotient is positive. When the signs are different, the product/quotient is negative.

$6 \times 7 = 42$ and $-6 \times (-7) = 42$
$-6 \times 7 = -42$ and $6 \times (-7) = -42$
$96 \div 8 = 12$ and $-96 \div (-8) = 12$
$-96 \div 8 = -12$ and $96 \div (-8) = -12$

6. How to plot points on the NUMBER LINE

To plot the point 4.5 on the number line, start at 0, go right to 4.5, halfway between 4 and 5.

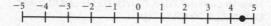

To plot the point −2.5 on the number line, start at 0, go left to −2.5, halfway between −2 and −3.

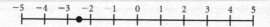

7. How to plug a number into an ALGEBRAIC EXPRESSION

To evaluate an algebraic expression, choose numbers for the variables or use the numbers assigned to the variables.

Evaluate $4np + 1$ when $n = -4$ and $p = 3$.

$4np + 1 = 4(-4)(3) + 1 = -48 + 1 = -47$

8. How to SOLVE a simple LINEAR EQUATION

Use algebra to isolate the variable. Do the same steps to both sides of the equation.

$$28 = -3x - 5$$
$$28 + 5 = -3x - 5 + 5 \qquad \text{Add 5.}$$
$$33 = -3x$$
$$\frac{33}{-3} = \frac{-3x}{-3} \qquad \text{Divide by } -3.$$
$$-11 = x$$

9. How to add and subtract LINE SEGMENTS

If $AB = 6$ and $BC = 8$, then $AC = 6 + 8 = 14$.
If $AC = 14$ and $BC = 8$, then $AB = 14 - 8 = 6$.

10. How to find the THIRD ANGLE of a TRIANGLE, given the other two angles

Use the fact that the sum of the measures of the interior angles of a triangle always sum to 180°.

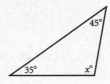

$$35 + 45 + x = 180$$
$$80 + x = 180$$
$$x = 100$$

MATH

LEVEL 2

11. How to use PEMDAS

When you're given a complex arithmetic expression, it's important to know the order of operations. Just remember PEMDAS (as in "Please excuse my dear Aunt Sally"). What PEMDAS means is this: Clean up **Parentheses** first (nested sets of parentheses are worked from the innermost set to the outermost set.); then deal with **Exponents** (or **Radicals**); then do the **Multiplication** and **Division** together, going from left to right; and finally do the **Addition** and **Subtraction** together, again going from left to right.

Example:

$$9 - 2 \times (5 - 3)^2 + 6 \div 3 =$$

Begin with the parentheses:

$$9 - 2 \times (2)^2 + 6 \div 3 =$$

Then do the exponent:

$$9 - 2 \times 4 + 6 \div 3 =$$

Now do multiplication and division from left to right:

$$9 - 8 + 2 =$$

Finally, do addition and subtraction from left to right:

$$1 + 2 = 3$$

12. How to use the PERCENT FORMULA

Identify the part, the percent, and the whole.

$$Part = Percent \times Whole$$

Find the part.

Example:

What is 12 percent of 25?

Setup:

$$Part = \frac{12}{100} \times 25 = \frac{300}{100} = 3$$

Find the percent.

Example:

45 is what percent of 9?

Setup:

$$45 = \frac{percent}{100} \times 9$$

$$\frac{45}{9} \times 100\% = 500\%$$

Find the whole.

Example:

15 is $\frac{3}{5}$ percent of what number?

Setup:

$$15 = \frac{3}{5}\left(\frac{1}{100}\right) \times Whole$$

$$15 = \frac{3}{500} \times Whole$$

$$Whole = 15\left(\frac{500}{3}\right) = \frac{7,500}{3} = 2,500$$

13. How to use the PERCENT INCREASE/ DECREASE FORMULAS

Identify the original whole and the amount of increase/decrease.

$$\text{Percent increase} = \frac{\text{Amount of increase}}{\text{Original whole}} \times 100\%$$

$$\text{Percent decrease} = \frac{\text{Amount of decrease}}{\text{Original whole}} \times 100\%$$

Example:

The price goes up from $80 to $100. What is the percent increase?

Setup:

$$\text{Percent increase} = \frac{20}{80} \times 100\%$$
$$= 0.25 \times 100\% = 25\%$$

14. How to predict whether a sum, difference, or product will be ODD or EVEN

Don't bother memorizing the rules. Just take simple numbers like 2 for even numbers and 3 for odd numbers and see what happens.

Example:

If m is even and n is odd, is the product mn odd or even?

Setup:

Say $m = 2$ and $n = 3$.
2×3 is even, so mn is even.

MATH

15. How to recognize MULTIPLES OF 2, 3, 4, 5, 6, 9, 10, and 12

2: Last digit is even

3: Sum of digits is a multiple of 3

4: Last two digits are a multiple of 4

5: Last digit is 5 or 0

6: Sum of digits is a multiple of 3, and last digit is even

9: Sum of digits is a multiple of 9

10: Last digit is 0

12: Sum of digits is a multiple of 3, and last two digits are a multiple of 4

16. How to find a COMMON FACTOR of two numbers

Break both numbers down to their prime factors to see which they have in common. Then multiply the shared prime factors to find all common factors.

Example:

What factors greater than 1 do 135 and 225 have in common?

Setup:

First find the prime factors of 135 and 225;
$135 = 3 \times 3 \times 3 \times 5$, and $225 = 3 \times 3 \times 5 \times 5$. The numbers share $3 \times 3 \times 5$ in common. Thus, aside from 3 and 5, the remaining common factors can be found by multiplying 3, 3, and 5 in every possible combination: $3 \times 3 = 9$, $3 \times 5 = 15$, and $3 \times 3 \times 5 = 45$. To summarize, the common factors of 135 and 225 are 3, 5, 9, 15, and 45.

MATH

17. How to find a COMMON MULTIPLE of two numbers

The product of two numbers is the easiest common multiple to find, but it is not always the least common multiple.

Example:

What is the least common multiple of 28 and 42?

Setup:

$$28 = 2 \times 2 \times 7$$
$$42 = 2 \times 3 \times 7$$

The LCM can be found by finding the prime factorization of each number, then seeing the greatest number of times each factor is used. Multiply each prime factor the greatest number of times it appears.

In 28, 2 is used twice. In 42, 2 is used once. In 28, 7 is used once. In 42, 7 is used once, and 3 is used once. So you multiply each factor the greatest number of times it appears in a prime factorization:

$$LCM = 2 \times 2 \times 3 \times 7 = 84$$

18. How to find the AVERAGE or ARITHMETIC MEAN

$$Average = \frac{Sum\ of\ terms}{Number\ of\ terms}$$

Example:

What is the average of 3, 4, and 8?

Setup:

$$Average = \frac{3 + 4 + 8}{3} = \frac{15}{3} = 5$$

MATH

19. How to use the AVERAGE to find the SUM

$$Sum = (Average) \times (Number\ of\ terms)$$

Example:

17.5 is the average (arithmetic mean) of 24 numbers.

What is the sum of the 24 numbers?

Setup:

$$Sum = 17.5 \times 24 = 420$$

20. How to find the AVERAGE of CONSECUTIVE NUMBERS

The average of evenly spaced numbers is simply the average of the smallest number and the largest number. The average of all the integers from 13 to 77, for example, is the same as the average of 13 and 77:

$$\frac{13 + 77}{2} = \frac{90}{2} = 45$$

21. How to COUNT CONSECUTIVE NUMBERS

The number of integers from A to B inclusive is $B - A + 1$.

Example:

How many integers are there from 73 through 419, inclusive?

Setup:

$$419 - 73 + 1 = 347$$

22. How to find the SUM OF CONSECUTIVE NUMBERS

Sum = (Average) × *(Number of terms)*

Example:

What is the sum of the integers from 10 through 50, inclusive?

Setup:

Average = (10 + 50) ÷ 2 = 30
Number of terms = 50 − 10 + 1 = 41
Sum = 30 × 41 = 1,230

23. How to find the MEDIAN

Put the numbers in numerical order and take the middle number.

Example:

What is the median of 88, 86, 57, 94, and 73?

Setup:

First, put the numbers in numerical order, then take the middle number:

$$57, 73, 86, 88, 94$$

The median is 86.

In a set with an even number of numbers, take the average of the two in the middle.

Example:

What is the median of 88, 86, 57, 73, 94, and 100?

Setup:

First, put the numbers in numerical order.

$$57, 73, 86, 88, 94, 100$$

Because 86 and 88 are the two numbers in the middle:

$$(86 + 88) ÷ 2 = 174 ÷ 2 = 87 \text{ is the median.}$$

24. How to find the MODE

Take the number that appears most often. For example, if your test scores were 88, 57, 68, 85, 98, 93, 93, 84, and 81, the mode of the scores would be 93 because it appears more often than any other score. (If there's a tie for most often, then there's more than one mode. If there is only one of each number in a set, there is no mode.)

25. How to find the RANGE

Take the positive difference between the greatest and least values. Using the example under "How to find the MODE" above, if your test scores were 88, 57, 68, 85, 98, 93, 93, 84, and 81, the range of the scores would be 41, the greatest value minus the least value ($98 - 57 = 41$).

26. How to use actual numbers to determine a RATIO

To find a ratio, put the number associated with *of* on the top and the word associated with *to* on the bottom.

$$Ratio = \frac{of}{to}$$

The ratio of 20 oranges to 12 apples is $\frac{20}{12}$, or $\frac{5}{3}$. Ratios should always be reduced to lowest terms.

. How to use a ratio to determine an ACTUAL NUMBER

Set up a proportion using the given ratio.

Example:

The ratio of boys to girls is 3 to 4. If there are 135 boys, how many girls are there?

Setup:

$$\frac{3}{4} = \frac{135}{g}$$
$$3 \times g = 4 \times 135$$
$$3g = 540$$
$$g = 180$$

28. How to use actual numbers to determine a RATE

Identify the quantities and the units to be compared. Keep the units straight.

Example:

Anders typed 9,450 words in $3\frac{1}{2}$ hours. What was his rate in words per minute?

Setup:

First convert $3\frac{1}{2}$ hours to 210 minutes. Then set up the rate with words on top and minutes on bottom (because "per" means "divided by"):

$$\frac{9,450 \text{ words}}{210 \text{ minutes}} = 45 \text{ words per minute}$$

29. How to deal with TABLES, GRAPHS, AND CHARTS

Read the question and all labels carefully. Ignore extraneous information and zero in on what the question asks for. Take advantage of the spread in the answer choices by approximating the answer whenever possible and choosing the answer choice closest to your approximation.

MATH

MATH

30. How to count the NUMBER OF POSSIBILITIES

You can use multiplication to find the number of possibilities when items can be arranged in various ways.

Example:

How many three-digit numbers can be formed with the digits 1, 3, and 5 each used only once?

Setup:

Look at each digit individually. The first digit (or, the hundreds digit) has three possible numbers to plug in: 1, 3, or 5. The second digit (or, the tens digit) has two possible numbers, since one has already been plugged in. The last digit (or, the ones digit) has only one remaining possible number. Multiply the possibilities together: $3 \times 2 \times 1 = 6$.

31. How to calculate a simple PROBABILITY

$$Probability = \frac{Number\ of\ favorable\ outcomes}{Total\ number\ of\ possible\ outcomes}$$

Example:

What is the probability of throwing a 5 on a fair six-sided die?

Setup:

There is one favorable outcome—throwing a 5. There are 6 possible outcomes—one for each side of the die.

$$Probability = \frac{1}{6}$$

32. How to work with new SYMBOLS

If you see a symbol you've never seen before, don't be alarmed. It's just a made-up symbol whose operation is defined by the problem. Everything you need to know is in the question stem. Just follow the instructions.

33. How to SIMPLIFY BINOMIALS

A binomial is a sum or difference of two terms. To simplify two binomials that are multiplied together use the FOIL method. Multiply the First terms, then the Outer terms, followed by the Inner terms and the Last terms. Lastly, combine like terms.

Example:

$$(3x + 5)(x - 1) =$$
$$3x^2 - 3x + 5x - 5 =$$
$$3x^2 + 2x - 5$$

34. How to FACTOR certain POLYNOMIALS

A polynomial is an expression consisting of the sum of two or more terms, where at least one of the terms is a variable.

Learn to spot these classic equations.

$$ab + ac = a(b + c)$$
$$a^2 + 2ab + b^2 = (a + b)^2$$
$$a^2 - 2ab + b^2 = (a - b)^2$$
$$a^2 - b^2 = (a - b)(a + b)$$

35. How to solve for one variable IN TERMS OF ANOTHER

To find x "in terms of" y, isolate x on one side, leaving y as the only variable on the other.

MATH

36. How to solve an INEQUALITY

Treat it much like an equation—adding, subtracting, multiplying, and dividing both sides by the same thing. Just remember to reverse the inequality sign if you multiply or divide by a negative quantity.

Example:

Rewrite $7 - 3x > 2$ in its simplest form.

Setup:

$$7 - 3x > 2$$

First, subtract 7 from both sides:

$$7 - 3x - 7 > 2 - 7$$

So $-3x > -5$.

Now divide both sides by -3, remembering to reverse the inequality sign:

$$x < \frac{5}{3}$$

37. How to handle ABSOLUTE VALUES

The *absolute value* of a number n, denoted by $|n|$, is defined as n if $n \geq 0$ and $-n$ if $n < 0$. The absolute value of a number is the distance from zero to the number on the number line. The absolute value of a number or expression is always positive.

$$|-5| = 5$$

If $|x| = 3$, then x could be 3 or -3.

Example:

If $|x - 3| < 2$, what is the range of possible values for x?

Setup:

Represent the possible range for $x - 3$ on a number line.

$|x - 3| < 2$, so $(x - 3) < 2$ and $(x - 3) > -2$

$x - 3 < 2$ and $x - 3 > -2$

$x < 2 + 3$ and $x > -2 + 3$

$x < 5$ and $x > 1$

So $1 < x < 5$.

38. How to TRANSLATE ENGLISH INTO ALGEBRA

Look for the keywords and systematically turn phrases into algebraic expressions and sentences into equations.

Here's a table of keywords that you may have to translate into mathematical terms:

Operation	Keywords
Addition	sum, plus, and, added to, more than, increased by, combined with, exceeds, total, greater than
Subtraction	difference between, minus, subtracted from, decreased by, diminished by, less than, reduced by
Multiplication	of, product, times, multiplied by, twice, double, triple, half
Division	quotient, divided by, per, out of, ratio of ___ to ___
Equals	equals, is, was, will be, the result is, adds up to, costs, is the same as

MATH

39. How to find an ANGLE formed by INTERSECTING LINES

Vertical angles are equal. Angles along a line add up to 180°.

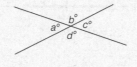

$$a = c$$
$$b = d$$
$$a + b = 180°$$
$$a + b + c + d = 360°$$

40. How to find an angle formed by a TRANSVERSAL across PARALLEL LINES

All the acute angles are equal. All the obtuse angles are equal. An acute plus an obtuse equals 180°.

Example:

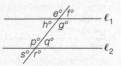

ℓ_1 is parallel to ℓ_2

$$e = g = p = r$$
$$f = h = q = s$$
$$e + q = g + s = 180°$$

41. How to find the AREA of a TRIANGLE

$$Area = \frac{1}{2}(base)(height)$$

Base and height must be perpendicular to each other. Height is measured by drawing a perpendicular line segment from the base—which can be any side of the triangle—to the angle opposite the base.

Example:

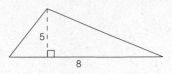

Setup:

$$Area = \frac{1}{2}(8)(5) = 20$$

42. How to work with ISOSCELES TRIANGLES

Isosceles triangles have two equal sides and two equal angles. If a GRE question tells you that a triangle is isoceles, you can bet that you'll need to use that information to find the length of a side or a measure of an angle.

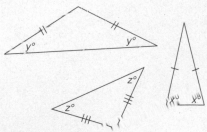

MATH

43. How to work with EQUILATERAL TRIANGLES

Equilateral triangles have three equal sides and three 60° angles. If a GRE question tells you that a triangle is equilateral, you can bet that you'll need to use that information to find the length of a side or a measure of an angle.

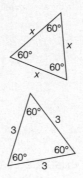

MATH

44. How to work with SIMILAR TRIANGLES

In similar triangles, corresponding angles are equal, and corresponding sides are proportional. If a GRE question tells you that triangles are
similar, use the properties of similar triangles to find the length of a
side or the measure of an angle.

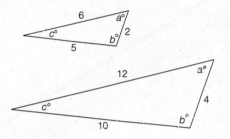

45. How to find the HYPOTENUSE or a LEG
of a RIGHT TRIANGLE

For all right triangles, Pythagorean theorem: $a^2 + b^2 = c^2$, where a and
b are the legs and c is the hypotenuse.

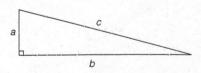

MATH

46. How to spot SPECIAL RIGHT TRIANGLES

3:4:5

5:12:13

30°-60°-90°

45°-45°-90°

These numbers (3, 4, 5 and 5, 12, 13) represent the ratio of the side
lengths of these triangles.

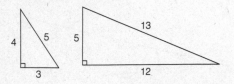

Likewise, the numbers 1, $\sqrt{3}$, 2 and 1, 1, $\sqrt{2}$ represent the ratios of the
side lengths of these special triangles.

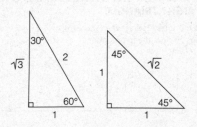

MATH

47. How to find the PERIMETER of a RECTANGLE

Perimeter = 2(length + width)

Example:

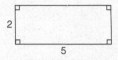

Setup:

Perimeter = 2(2 + 5) = 14

48. How to find the AREA of a RECTANGLE

Area = (length)(width)

Example:

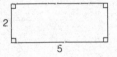

Setup:

Area = 2 × 5 = 10

MATH

49. How to find the AREA of a SQUARE

$$Area = (side)^2$$

Example:

Setup:

$$Area = 3^2 = 9$$

50. How to find the AREA of a PARALLELOGRAM

$$Area = (base)(height)$$

Example:

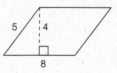

Setup:

$$Area = 8 \times 4 = 32$$

MATH

51. How to find the AREA of a TRAPEZOID

A trapezoid is a quadrilateral having only two parallel sides. You can always drop a perpendicular line or two to break the figure into a rectangle and a triangle or two triangles. Use the area formulas for those familiar shapes. Alternatively, you could apply the general formula for the area of a trapezoid:

$$Area = (average\ of\ parallel\ sides) \times (height)$$

Example:

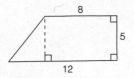

Setup:

Area of rectangle $= 8 \times 5 = 40$

Area of triangle $= \frac{1}{2}(4 \times 5) = 10$

Area of trapezoid $= 40 + 10 = 50$
or Area of trapezoid $= \left(\frac{8 + 12}{2}\right) \times 5 = 50$

MATH

52. How to find the CIRCUMFERENCE of a CIRCLE

Circumference = 2πr, where r is the radius.

Circumference = πd, where d is the diameter.

Example:

Setup:

$$Circumference = 2\pi(5) = 10\pi$$

53. How to find the AREA of a CIRCLE

Area = πr², where r is the radius.

Example:

Setup:

$$Area = \pi \times 5^2 = 25\pi$$

54. How to find the DISTANCE BETWEEN POINTS on the coordinate plane

If two points have the same *x* coordinates or the same *y* coordinates—that is, they make a line segment that is parallel to an axis—all you have to do is subtract the numbers that are different. Just remember that distance is always positive.

Example:

What is the distance from (2, 3) to (−7, 3)?

Setup:

The *y*'s are the same, so just subtract the *x*'s:
$2 − (−7) = 9$.

If the points have different *x* coordinates and different *y* coordinates, make a right triangle and use the Pythagorean theorem or apply the special right triangle attributes if applicable.

Example:

What is the distance from (2, 3) to (−1, −1)?

Setup:

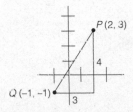

It's a 3:4:5 triangle!

$PQ = 5$

55. How to find the SLOPE of a LINE

$$Slope = \frac{rise}{run} = \frac{change\ in\ y}{change\ in\ x}$$

Example:

What is the slope of the line that contains the points (1, 2) and (4, −5)?

Setup:

$$Slope = \frac{-5 - 2}{4 - 1} = \frac{-7}{3}$$

MATH

LEVEL 3

56. How to determine COMBINED PERCENT INCREASE/DECREASE

Start with 100 as a starting value.

Example:

A price rises by 10 percent one year and by 20 percent the next. What's the combined percent increase?

Setup:

Say the original price is $100.

Year one:
$100 + (10% of 100) = 100 + 10 = 110

Year two:
110 + (20% of 110) = 110 + 22 = 132

From 100 to 132—that's a 32 percent increase.

57. How to find the ORIGINAL WHOLE before percent increase/decrease

Think of a 15 percent increase over x as 1.15x and set up an equation.

Example:

After decreasing by 5 percent, the population is now 57,000. What was the original population?

Setup:

0.95 × (Original population) = 57,000
Divide both sides by 0.95.
Original population = 57,000 ÷ 0.95 = 60,000

MATH

58. How to solve a SIMPLE INTEREST problem

With simple interest, the interest is computed on the principal only and is given by:

$$interest = (principal) \times (interest\ rate^*) \times (time^{**})$$

* expressed as a decimal
** expressed in years or fraction of a year

Example:

If $12,000 is invested at 6 percent simple annual interest, how much interest is earned after 9 months?

Setup:

$$(12,000) \times (0.06) \times \left(\frac{9}{12}\right) = \$540$$

59. How to solve a COMPOUND INTEREST problem

If interest is compounded, the interest is computed on the principal as well as on any interest earned. To compute compound interest:

$$(Final\ balance) = (Principal) \times \left(1 + \frac{Interest\ rate}{C}\right)^{(time)(C)}$$

where C = the number of times compounded annually

Example:

If $10,000 is invested at 8 percent annual interest, compounded semi-annually, what is the balance after 1 year?

Setup:

Final balance

$$= (10,000) \times \left(1 + \frac{0.08}{2}\right)^{(1)(2)}$$
$$= (10,000) \times (1.04)^2$$
$$= \$10,816$$

60. How to solve a REMAINDERS problem

Pick a number that fits the given conditions and see what happens.

Example:

When *n* is divided by 7, the remainder is 5. What is the remainder when 2*n* is divided by 7?

Setup:

Find a number that leaves a remainder of 5 when divided by 7. You can find such a number by taking any multiple of 7 and adding 5 to it.

A good choice would be 12. If *n* = 12, then 2*n* = 24, which when divided by 7 leaves a remainder of 3.

61. How to solve a DIGITS problem

Use a little logic—and some trial and error.

Example:

If *A*, *B*, *C*, and *D* represent distinct digits in the addition problem below, what is the value of *D*?

$$
\begin{array}{r}
AB \\
+\ BA \\
\hline
CDC
\end{array}
$$

Setup:

Two 2-digit numbers will add up to at most something in the 100s, so *C* = 1. *B* plus *A* in the units column gives a 1, and since *A* and *B* in the tens column don't add up to *C*, it can't simply be that *B* + *A* = 1. It must be that *B* + *A* = 11, and a 1 gets carried. In fact, *A* and *B* can be any pair of digits that add up to 11 (3 and 8, 4 and 7, etc.), but it doesn't matter what they are: they always give you the same value for *D*, which is 2:

$$
\begin{array}{r}
47 \\
+\ 74 \\
\hline
121
\end{array}
\qquad
\begin{array}{r}
83 \\
+\ 38 \\
\hline
121
\end{array}
$$

MATH

62. How to find a WEIGHTED AVERAGE

Give each term the appropriate "weight."

Example:

The girls' average score is 30. The boys' average score is 24. If there are twice as many boys as girls, what is the overall average?

Setup:

Weighted avg. = $\frac{1 \times 30 + 2 \times 24}{3} = \frac{78}{3} = 26$

HINT:

Don't just average the averages.

63. How to find the NEW AVERAGE when a number is added or deleted

Use the sum of the terms of the old average to help you find the new average.

Example:

Michael's average score after four tests is 80. If he scores 100 on the fifth test, what's his new average?

Setup:

Find the original sum from the original average:

$$\text{Original sum} = 4 \times 80 = 320$$

Add the fifth score to make the new sum:

$$\text{New sum} = 320 + 100 = 420$$

Find the new average from the new sum:

$$\text{New average} = \frac{420}{5} = 84$$

64. How to use the ORIGINAL AVERAGE and NEW AVERAGE to figure out WHAT WAS ADDED OR DELETED

Use the sums.

$$\text{Number added} = (\text{new sum}) - (\text{original sum})$$
$$\text{Number deleted} = (\text{original sum}) - (\text{new sum})$$

Example:

The average of five numbers is 2. After one number is deleted, the new average is -3. What number was deleted?

Setup:

Find the original sum from the original average:

$$\text{Original sum} = 5 \times 2 = 10$$

Find the new sum from the new average:

$$\text{New sum} = 4 \times (-3) = -12$$

The difference between the original sum and the new sum is the answer.

$$\text{Number deleted} = 10 - (-12) = 22$$

MATH

65. How to find an AVERAGE RATE

Find the ratio of totals.

$$\text{Average } A \text{ per } B = \frac{\text{Total } A}{\text{Total } B}$$

Example:

If the first 500 pages have an average of 150 words per page, and the remaining 100 pages have an average of 450 words per page, what is the average number of words per page for the entire 600 pages?

Setup:

Total pages = 500 + 100 = 600
Total words = (500 × 150) + (100 × 450)
                = 120,000

$$\text{Average words per page} = \frac{120,000}{600} = 200$$

To find an average speed, you also find the ratio of totals.

$$\text{Average speed} = \frac{\text{Total distance}}{\text{Time}}$$

Example:

Rosa drove 120 miles one way at an average speed of 40 miles per hour and returned by the same 120-mile route at an average speed of 60 miles per hour. What was Rosa's average speed for the entire 240-mile round trip?

Setup:

To drive 120 miles at 40 mph takes 3 hours. To return at 60 mph takes 2 hours. The total time, then, is 5 hours.

$$\text{Average speed} = \frac{240 \text{ miles}}{5 \text{ hours}} = 48 \text{ mph}$$

MATH

66. How to solve a COMBINED WORK PROBLEM

In a combined work problem, you are given the rate at which people or machines perform work individually and asked to compute the rate at which they work together (or vice versa). The work formula states: *The inverse of the time it would take everyone working together equals the sum of the inverses of the times it would take each working individually.* In other words:

$$\frac{1}{r} + \frac{1}{s} = \frac{1}{t}$$

where r and s are, for example, the number of hours it would take Rebecca and Sam, respectively, to complete a job working by themselves, and t is the number of hours it would take the two of them working together. Remember that all these variables must stand for units of TIME and must all refer to the amount of time it takes to do the same task.

Example:

If it takes Joe 4 hours to paint a room and Pete twice as long to paint the same room, how long would it take the two of them, working together, to paint the same room, if each of them works at his respective individual rate?

Setup:

Joe takes 4 hours, so Pete takes 8 hours; thus:

$$\frac{1}{4} + \frac{1}{8} = \frac{1}{t}$$
$$\frac{2}{8} + \frac{1}{8} = \frac{1}{t}$$
$$\frac{3}{8} = \frac{1}{t}$$
$$t = \frac{1}{\left(\frac{3}{8}\right)} = \frac{8}{3}$$

So it would take them $\frac{8}{3}$ hours, or 2 hours 40 minutes, to paint the room together.

MATH

67. How to determine a COMBINED RATIO

Multiply one or both ratios by whatever you need to in order to get the terms they have in common to match.

Example:

The ratio of *a* to *b* is 7:3. The ratio of *b* to *c* is 2:5. What is the ratio of *a* to *c* ?

Setup:

Multiply each member of $a:b$ by 2 and multiply each member of $b:c$ by 3, and you get $a:b = 14:6$ and $b:c = 6:15$. Now that the *b*'s match, you can write $a:b:c = 14:6:15$ and then say $a:c = 14:15$.

68. How to solve a DILUTION or MIXTURE problem

In dilution or mixture problems, you have to determine the characteristics of a resulting mixture when different substances are combined. Or, alternatively, you have to determine how to combine different substances to produce a desired mixture. There are two approaches to such problems—the straightforward setup and the balancing method.

Example:

If 5 pounds of raisins that cost $1 per pound are mixed with 2 pounds of almonds that cost $2.40 per pound, what is the cost per pound of the resulting mixture?

Setup:

The straightforward setup:

$(\$1)(5) + (\$2.40)(2) = \$9.80 =$ total cost for 7 pounds of the mixture

The cost per pound is $\$\frac{9.80}{7} = \$1.40$.

Example:

How many liters of a solution that is 10 percent alcohol by volume must be added to 2 liters of a solution that is 50 percent alcohol by volume to create a solution that is 15 percent alcohol by volume?

Setup:

The balancing method: Make the weaker and stronger (or cheaper and more expensive, etc.) substances balance. That is, (percent difference between the weaker solution and the desired solution) $\times$ (amount of weaker solution) = (percent difference between the stronger solution and the desired solution) $\times$ (amount of stronger solution). Make n the amount, in liters, of the weaker solution.

$$n(15 - 10) = 2(50 - 15)$$
$$5n = 2(35)$$
$$n = \frac{70}{5} = 14$$

So 14 liters of the 10 percent solution must be added to the original, stronger solution.

MATH

MATH

69. How to solve a GROUP problem involving BOTH/NEITHER

Some GRE word problems involve two groups with overlapping members and possibly elements that belong to neither group. It's easy to identify this type of question because the words *both* and/or *neither* appear in the question. These problems are quite workable if you just memorize the following formula:

$$Group\ 1 + Group\ 2 + Neither - Both = Total$$

Example:

Of the 120 students at a certain language school, 65 are studying French, 51 are studying Spanish, and 53 are studying neither language. How many are studying both French and Spanish?

Setup:

$$65 + 51 + 53 - Both = 120$$
$$169 - Both = 120$$
$$Both = 49$$

70. How to solve a GROUP problem involving EITHER/OR CATEGORIES

Other GRE word problems involve groups with distinct "either/or" categories (male/female, blue-collar/white-collar, etc.). The key to solving this type of problem is to organize the information in a grid.

Example:

At a certain professional conference with 130 attendees, 94 of the attendees are doctors, and the rest are dentists. If 48 of the attendees are women and $\frac{1}{4}$ of the dentists in attendance are women, how many of the attendees are male doctors?

Setup:

To complete the grid, use the information in the problem, making each row and column add up to the corresponding total:

	Doctors	Dentists	Total
Male	55	27	82
Female		9	48
Total	94	36	130

After you've filled in the information from the question, use simple arithmetic to fill in the remaining boxes until you get the number you are looking for—in this case, that 55 of the attendees are male doctors.

MATH

71. How to work with FACTORIALS

You may see a problem involving factorial notation. If n is an integer greater than 1, then n factorial, denoted by $n!$, is defined as the product of all the integers from 1 to n. In other words:

$$2! = 2 \times 1 = 2$$
$$3! = 3 \times 2 \times 1 = 6$$
$$4! = 4 \times 3 \times 2 \times 1 = 24, \text{ etc.}$$

By definition, $0! = 1$.

Also note: $6! = 6 \times 5! = 6 \times 5 \times 4!$, etc. Most GRE factorial problems test your ability to factor and/or cancel.

Example:

$$\frac{8!}{6! \times 2!} = \frac{8 \times 7 \times 6!}{6! \times 2 \times 1} = 28$$

72. How to solve a PERMUTATION problem

Factorials are useful for solving questions about permutations (i.e., the number of ways to arrange elements sequentially). For instance, to figure out how many ways there are to arrange 7 items along a shelf, you would multiply the number of possibilities for the first position times the number of possibilities remaining for the second position, and so on—in other words: $7 \times 6 \times 5 \times 4 \times 3 \times 2 \times 1$, or $7!$.

If you're asked to find the number of ways to arrange a smaller group that's being drawn from a larger group, you can either apply logic, or you can use the permutation formula:

$$_nP_k = \frac{n!}{(n - k)!}$$

where n = (the number in the larger group) and

k = (the number you're arranging)

Example:

Five runners run in a race. The runners who come in first, second, and third place will win gold, silver, and bronze medals respectively. How many possible outcomes for gold, silver, and bronze medal winners are there?

Setup:

Any of the 5 runners could come in first place, leaving 4 runners who could come in second place, leaving 3 runners who could come in third place, for a total of $5 \times 4 \times 3 = 60$ possible outcomes for gold, silver, and bronze medal winners. Or, using the formula:

$$_5P_3 = \frac{5!}{(5-3)!} = \frac{5!}{2!} = \frac{5 \times 4 \times 3 \times \cancel{2} \times \cancel{1}}{\cancel{2} \times \cancel{1}}$$
$$= 5 \times 4 \times 3 = 60$$

73. How to solve a COMBINATION problem

If the order or arrangement of the smaller group that's being drawn from the larger group does NOT matter, you are looking for the numbers of combinations, and a different formula is called for:

$$_nC_k = \frac{n!}{k!(n-k)!}$$

where $n =$ (the number in the larger group) and
$k =$ (the number you're choosing)

Example:

How many different ways are there to choose 3 delegates from 8 possible candidates?

Setup:

$$_8C_3 = \frac{8!}{3!(8-3)!} = \frac{8!}{3! \times 5!}$$

$$= \frac{8 \times 7 \times \cancel{6} \times \cancel{5} \times \cancel{4} \times \cancel{3} \times \cancel{2} \times \cancel{1}}{\cancel{3} \times \cancel{2} \times 1 \times \cancel{5} \times \cancel{4} \times \cancel{3} \times \cancel{2} \times \cancel{1}}$$
$$= 8 \times 7 = 56$$

So there are 56 different possible combinations.

74. How to solve PROBABILITY problems where probabilities must be multiplied

Suppose that a random process is performed. Then there is a set of possible outcomes that can occur. An event is a set of possible outcomes. We are concerned with the probability of events.

When all the outcomes are all equally likely, the basic probability formula is:

$$Probability = \frac{Number\ of\ favorable\ outcomes}{Number\ of\ possible\ outcomes}$$

Many more difficult probability questions involve finding the probability that several events occur. Let's consider first the case of the probability that two events occur. Call these two events A and B. The probability that both events occur is the probability that event A occurs multiplied by the probability that event B occurs given that event A occurred. The probability that B occurs given that A occurs is called the conditional probability that B occurs given that A occurs. Except when events A and B do not depend on one another, the probability that B occurs given that A occurs is not the same as the probability that B occurs.

The probability that three events A, B, and C occur is the probability that A occurs multiplied by the conditional probability that B occurs given that A occurred multiplied by the conditional probability that C occurs given that both A and B have occurred.

This can be generalized to any number of events, where the number of events is an integer greater than 3.

Example:

If 2 students are chosen at random to run an errand from a class with 5 girls and 5 boys, what is the probability that both students chosen will be girls?

Setup:

The probability that the first student chosen will be a girl is $\frac{5}{10}$ $= \frac{1}{2}$, and since there would be 4 girls and 5 boys left out of 9 students, the probability that the second student chosen will be a girl (given that the first student chosen is a girl) is $\frac{4}{9}$. Thus, the probability that both students chosen will be girls is $\frac{1}{2} \times \frac{4}{9} = \frac{2}{9}$. There was conditional probability here because the probability of choosing the second girl was affected by another girl being chosen first.

Now let's consider another example where a random process is repeated.

Example:

If a fair coin is tossed 4 times, what's the probability that at least 3 of the 4 tosses will be heads?

Setup:

There are 2 possible outcomes for each toss, so after 4 tosses, there are $2 \times 2 \times 2 \times 2 = 16$ possible outcomes.

We can list the different possible sequences where at least 3 of the 4 tosses are heads. These sequences are

HHHT
HHTH
HTHH
THHH
HHHH

Thus, the probability that at least 3 of the 4 tosses will come up heads is:

$$\frac{\text{Number of favorable outcomes}}{\text{Number of possible outcomes}} = \frac{5}{16}$$

We could have also solved this question using the combinations formula. The probability of a head is $\frac{1}{2}$, and the probability of a tail is $\frac{1}{2}$. The probability of any particular sequence of heads and tails resulting from 4 tosses is $\frac{1}{2} \times \frac{1}{2} \times \frac{1}{2} \times \frac{1}{2}$, which is $\frac{1}{16}$. Suppose that the result each of the four tosses is recorded in each of the four spaces.

_____ _____ _____ _____

Thus, we would record an H for head or a T for tails in each of the 4 spaces.

The number of ways of having exactly 3 heads among the 4 tosses is the number of ways of choosing 3 of the 4 spaces above to record an H for heads.

The number of ways of choosing 3 of the 4 spaces is

$$_4C_3 = \frac{4!}{3!(4-3)!} = \frac{4!}{3!(1)!} = \frac{4 \times 3 \times 2 \times 1}{3 \times 2 \times 1 \times 1} = 4$$

The number of ways of having exactly 4 heads among the 4 tosses is 1.

If we use the combinations formula, using the definition that $0! = 1$, then

$$_4C_4 = \frac{4!}{4!(4-4)!} = \frac{4!}{4!(0)!}$$
$$= \frac{4 \times 3 \times 2 \times 1}{4 \times 3 \times 2 \times 1 \times 1} = 1$$

Thus, $_4C_3 = 4$ and $_4C_4 = 1$. So the number of different sequences containing at least 3 heads is $4 + 1 = 5$.

The probability of having at least 3 heads is $\frac{5}{16}$.

75. How to deal with STANDARD DEVIATION

Like mean, mode, median, and range, standard deviation is a term used to describe sets of numbers. Standard deviation is a measure of how spread out a set of numbers is (how much the numbers deviate from the mean). The greater the spread, the higher the standard deviation. You'll rarely have to calculate the standard deviation on Test Day (although this skill may be necessary for some high-difficulty questions). Here's how standard deviation is calculated:

- Find the average (arithmetic mean) of the set.
- Find the differences between the mean and each value in the set.
- Square each of the differences.

- Find the average of the squared differences.
- Take the positive square root of the average.

In addition to the occasional question that asks you to calculate standard deviation, you may also be asked to compare standard deviations between sets of data or otherwise demonstrate that you understand what standard deviation means. You can often handle these questions using estimation.

Example:

High temperatures, in degrees Fahrenheit, in two cities over five days:

September	1	2	3	4	5
City A	54	61	70	49	56
City B	62	56	60	67	65

For the five-day period listed, which city had the greater standard deviation in high temperatures?

Setup:

Even without trying to calculate them out, one can see that City A has the greater spread in temperatures and, therefore, the greater standard deviation in high temperatures. If you were to go ahead and calculate the standard deviations following the steps described above, you would find that the standard deviation in high temperatures for City A $= \sqrt{\frac{254}{5}} \approx 7.1$, while the standard deviation for City B $\approx \sqrt{\frac{74}{5}} \approx 3.8$.

76. How to MULTIPLY/DIVIDE VALUES WITH EXPONENTS/POWERS

Add/subtract the exponents.

Example:

$$x^a \times x^b = x^{a+b}$$
$$2^3 \times 2^4 = 2^7$$

Example:

$$\frac{x^c}{x^d} = x^{c-d}$$
$$\frac{5^6}{5^2} = 5^4$$

77. How to handle a value with an EXPONENT RAISED TO AN EXPONENT

Multiply the exponents.

Example:

$$(x^a)^b = x^{ab}$$
$$(3^4)^5 = 3^{20}$$

78. How to handle POWERS with a BASE of ZERO and POWERS with an EXPONENT of ZERO

Zero raised to any nonzero exponent equals zero.

Example:

$$0^4 = 0^{12} = 0^1 = 0$$

Any nonzero number raised to the exponent 0 equals 1.

Example:

$$3^0 = 15^0 = (0.34)^0 = (-345)^0 = \pi^0 = 1$$

The lone exception is 0 raised to the 0 power, which is *undefined*.

79. How to handle NEGATIVE POWERS

A number raised to the exponent $-x$ is the reciprocal of that number raised to the exponent x.

Example:

$$n^{-1} = \frac{1}{n}, n^{-2} = \frac{1}{n^2}, \text{ and so on.}$$

$$5^{-3} = \frac{1}{5^3} = \frac{1}{5 \times 5 \times 5} = \frac{1}{125}$$

80. How to handle FRACTIONAL POWERS

Fractional exponents relate to roots. For instance, $x^{\frac{1}{2}} = \sqrt{x}$.
Likewise, $x^{\frac{1}{3}} = \sqrt[3]{x}$, $x^{\frac{2}{3}} = \sqrt[3]{x^2}$, and so on.

Example:

$$(x^{-2})^{\frac{1}{2}} = x^{(-2)\left(\frac{1}{2}\right)} = x^{-1} = \frac{1}{x}$$
$$4^{\frac{1}{2}} = \sqrt{4} = 2$$

81. How to handle CUBE ROOTS

The cube root of x is just the number that when used as a factor 3 times (i.e., cubed) gives you x. Both positive and negative numbers have one and only one cube root, denoted by the symbol $\sqrt[3]{}$, and the cube root of a number is always the same sign as the number itself.

Example:

$$(-5) \times (-5) \times (-5) = -125, \text{ so } \sqrt[3]{-125}$$
$$= -5$$
$$\frac{1}{2} \times \frac{1}{2} \times \frac{1}{2} = \frac{1}{8}, \text{ so } \sqrt[3]{\frac{1}{8}} \to \frac{1}{2}$$

82. How to ADD, SUBTRACT, MULTIPLY, and DIVIDE ROOTS

You can add/subtract roots only when the parts inside the $\sqrt{}$ are identical.

Example:

$\sqrt{2} + 3\sqrt{2} = 4\sqrt{2}$
$\sqrt{2} - 3\sqrt{2} = -2\sqrt{2}$
$\sqrt{2} + \sqrt{3}$ cannot be combined.

To multiply/divide roots, deal with what's inside the $\sqrt{}$ and outside the $\sqrt{}$ separately.

Example:

$$(2\sqrt{3})(7\sqrt{5}) = (2 \times 7)(\sqrt{3 \times 5}) = 14\sqrt{15}$$

$$\frac{10\sqrt{21}}{5\sqrt{3}} = \frac{10}{5}\sqrt{\frac{21}{3}} = 2\sqrt{7}$$

83. How to SIMPLIFY A RADICAL

Look for factors of the number under the radical sign that are perfect squares; then find the square root of those perfect squares. Keep simplifying until the term with the square root sign is as simplified as possible: there are no other perfect square factors (4, 9, 16, 25, 36...) inside the $\sqrt{}$. Write the perfect squares as separate factors and "unsquare" them.

Example:

$$\sqrt{48} = \sqrt{16} \times \sqrt{3} = 4\sqrt{3}$$
$$\sqrt{180} = \sqrt{36} \times \sqrt{5} = 6\sqrt{5}$$

84. How to solve certain QUADRATIC EQUATIONS

Manipulate the equation (if necessary) into the "_____ = 0" form, factor the left side (reverse FOIL by finding two numbers whose product is the constant and whose sum is the coefficient of the term without the exponent), and break the quadratic into two simple expressions. Then find the value(s) for the variable that make either expression = 0.

Example:

$$x^2 + 6 = 5x$$
$$x^2 - 5x + 6 = 0$$
$$(x - 2)(x - 3) = 0$$
$$x - 2 = 0 \text{ or } x - 3 = 0$$
$$x = 2 \text{ or } 3$$

Example:

$$x^2 = 9$$
$$x = 3 \text{ or } -3$$

85. How to solve MULTIPLE EQUATIONS

When you see two equations with two variables on the GRE, they're probably easy to combine in such a way that you get something closer to what you're looking for.

Example:

If $5x - 2y = -9$ and $3y - 4x = 6$, what is the value of $x + y$?

Setup:

The question doesn't ask for x and y separately, so don't solve for them separately if you don't have to. Look what happens if you just rearrange a little and "add" the equations:

$$
\begin{aligned}
5x - 2y &= -9 \\
+[-4x + 3y &= 6] \\
\hline
x + y &= -3
\end{aligned}
$$

86. How to solve a SEQUENCE problem

The notation used in sequence problems scares many test takers, but these problems aren't as bad as they look. In a sequence problem, the nth term in the sequence is generated by performing an operation, which will be defined for you, on either n or on the previous term in the sequence. For instance, if you are referring to the fourth term in a sequence, it is called n_4 in sequence notation. Familiarize yourself with sequence notation, and you should have no problem.

Example:

What is the positive difference between the fifth and fourth terms in the sequence 0, 4, 18, ... whose nth term is $n^2(n - 1)$?

Setup:

Use the definition given to come up with the values for your terms:

$$n_5 = 5^2(5 - 1) = 25(4) = 100$$
$$n_4 = 4^2(4 - 1) = 16(3) = 48$$

So the positive difference between the fifth and fourth terms is $100 - 48 = 52$.

87. How to solve a FUNCTION problem

You may see function notation on the GRE. An algebraic expression of only one variable may be defined as a function, usually symbolized by f or g, of that variable.

Example:

What is the minimum value of x in the function $f(x) = x^2 - 1$?

Setup:

In the function $f(x) = x^2 - 1$, if x is 1, then $f(1) = 1^2 - 1 = 0$. In other words, by inputting 1 into the function, the output $f(x) = 0$. Every number inputted has one and only one output (although the reverse is not necessarily true). You're asked to find the minimum value, so how would you minimize the expression $f(x) = x^2 - 1$? Since x^2 cannot be negative, in this case $f(x)$ is minimized by making $x = 0$: $f(0) = 0^2 - 1 = -1$, so the minimum value of the function is -1.

88. How to handle GRAPHS of FUNCTIONS

You may see a problem that involves a function graphed onto the xy-coordinate plane, often called a "rectangular coordinate system" on the GRE. When graphing a function, the output, $f(x)$, becomes the y-coordinate. For example, in the previous example, $f(x) = x^2 - 1$, you've already determined 2 points, (1, 0) and (0, −1). If you were to keep plugging in numbers to determine more points and then plotted those points on the xy-coordinate plane, you would come up with something like this:

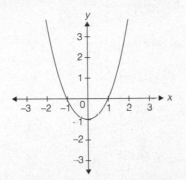

This curved line is called a *parabola*. In the event that you should see a parabola on the GRE (it could be upside down or more narrow or wider than the one shown), you will most likely be asked to choose which equation the parabola is describing. These questions can be surprisingly easy to answer. Pick out obvious points on the graph, such as (1, 0) and (0, −1) above, plug these values into the answer choices, and eliminate answer choices that don't jibe with those values until only one answer choice is left.

89. How to handle LINEAR EQUATIONS

You may also encounter linear equations on the GRE. A linear equation is often expressed in the form

$$y = mx + b, \text{ where}$$

m = the slope of the line = $\frac{rise}{run}$

b = the y-intercept (the point where the line crosses the y-axis)

For instance, a slope of 3 means that the line rises 3 steps for every 1 step it makes to the right. A line with positive slope slopes up from left to right. A line with negative slope slopes down from left to right. A slope of zero (e.g., $y = 5$) is a flat (horizontal) line.

Example:

The graph of the linear equation $y = -\frac{3}{4}x + 3$ is this:

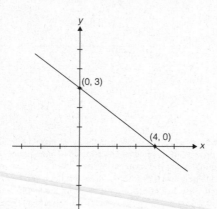

Note:

The equation could also be written in the form $3x + 4y = 12$, but this form does not readily describe the slope and y-intercept of the line.

To get a better handle on an equation written in this form, you can solve for y to write it in its more familiar form. Or, if you're asked to choose which equation the line is describing, you can pick obvious points, such as $(0, 3)$ and $(4, 0)$ in this example, and use these values to eliminate answer choices until only one answer is left.

90. How to find the x- and y-INTERCEPTS of a line

The x-intercept of a line is the value of x where the line crosses the x-axis. In other words, it's the value of x when $y = 0$. Likewise, the y-intercept is the value of y where the line crosses the y-axis (i.e., the value of y when $x = 0$). The y-intercept is also the value b when the equation is in the form $y = mx + b$. For instance, in the line shown in the previous example, the x-intercept is 4 and the y-intercept is 3.

91. How to find the MAXIMUM and MINIMUM lengths for a SIDE of a TRIANGLE

If you know n = the lengths of two sides of a triangle, you know that the third side is somewhere between the positive difference and the sum.

Example:

The length of one side of a triangle is 7. The length of another side is 3. What is the range of possible lengths for the third side?

Setup:

The third side is greater than the difference $(7 - 3 = 4)$ and less than the sum $(7 + 3 = 10)$.

92. How to find one angle or the sum of all the ANGLES of a REGULAR POLYGON

The term *regular* means all angles in the polygon are of equal measure.

Sum of the interior angles in a polygon with n sides =

$$(n - 2) \times 180$$

Degree measure of one angle in a regular polygon with n sides =

$$\frac{(n - 2) \times 180}{n}$$

Example:

What is the measure of one angle of a regular pentagon?

Setup:

Since a pentagon is a five-sided figure, plug $n = 5$ into the formula: Degree measure of one angle

$$= \frac{(5 - 2) \times 180}{5} = \frac{540}{5} = 108$$

93. How to find the LENGTH of an ARC

Think of an arc as a fraction of the circle's circumference. Use the measure of an interior angle of a circle, which has 360 degrees around the central point, to determine the length of an arc.

$$\text{Length of arc} = \frac{n}{360} \times 2\pi r$$

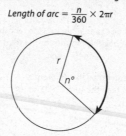

MATH

94. How to find the AREA of a SECTOR

Think of a sector as a fraction of the circle's area. Again, set up the interior angle measure as a fraction of 360, which is the degree measure of a circle a round the central point.

$$Area\ of\ sector = \frac{n}{360} \times \pi r^2$$

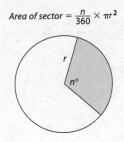

MATH

95. How to find the dimensions or area of an INSCRIBED or CIRCUMSCRIBED FIGURE

Look for the connection. Is the diameter of the circle the same as a side or a diagonal of the polygon?

Example:

If the area of the square is 36, what is the circumference of the circle?

Setup:

To get the circumference, you need the diameter or radius. The circle's diameter is also the square's diagonal. The diagonal of the square is $6\sqrt{2}$. This is because the diagonal of the square transforms it into two separate 45°-45°-90° triangles (see #46). So, the diameter of the circle is $6\sqrt{2}$.

$$\text{Circumference} = \pi(\text{diameter}) = 6\pi\sqrt{2}$$

96. How to find the VOLUME of a RECTANGULAR SOLID

Volume = length × width × height

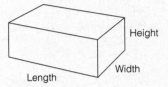

Height

Width

Length

MATH

97. How to find the SURFACE AREA of a RECTANGULAR SOLID

To find the surface area of a rectangular solid, you have to find the area of each face and add them together. Here's the formula:

Let l = length, w = width, h = height:

$$\text{Surface area} = 2(lw) + 2(wh) + 2(lh)$$

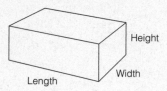

Height

Width

Length

98. How to find the DIAGONAL of a RECTANGULAR SOLID

Use the Pythagorean theorem twice, unless you spot "special" triangles.

Example:

What is the length of AG?

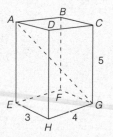

Setup:

Draw diagonal *AC*.

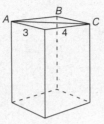

ABC is a 3:4:5 triangle, so *AC* = 5. Now look at triangle *ACG*:

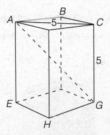

ACG is another special triangle, so you don't need to use the Pythagorean theorem. *ACG* is a 45°-45°-90° triangle, so $AG = 5\sqrt{2}$.

MATH

99. How to find the VOLUME of a CYLINDER

Volume = area of the base × height = $\pi r^2 h$

Example:

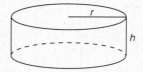

Let $r = 6$ and $h = 3$.

Setup:

$$\text{Volume} = \pi r^2 h = \pi (6^2)(3) = 108\pi$$

100. How to find the SURFACE AREA of a CYLINDER

Surface area = $2\pi r^2 + 2\pi rh$

Example:

Let $r = 3$ and $h = 4$.

Setup:

$$\begin{aligned}\text{Surface area} &= 2\pi r^2 + 2\pi rh \\ &= 2\pi(3)^2 + 2\pi(3)(4) \\ &= 18\pi + 24\pi = 42\pi\end{aligned}$$

INDEX

Index

Index

Index

Index